CHINESE PAPER FOLDING FOR BEGINNERS

Maying Soong

DOVER PUBLICATIONS, INC.
Mineola, New York

Published in Canada by General Publishing Company, Ltd., 895 Don Mills Road, 400-2 Park Centre, Toronto, Ontario M3C 1W3.
Published in the United Kingdom by David & Charles, Brunel House, Forde Close, Newton Abbot, Devon TQ12 4PU.

Bibliographical Note

This Dover edition, first published in 2001, is an unabridged republication of the work originally published in 1948 under the title *The Art of Chinese Paper Folding for Young and Old*.

Library of Congress Cataloging-in-Publication Data

Soong, Maying.
    [Art of Chinese paper folding for young and old]
    Chinese paper folding for beginners / Maying Soong.
       p. cm.
    Originally published: New York : Harcourt, Brace, 1948.
    ISBN 0-486-41806-5 (pbk.)
    1. Paper work. 2. Paper toys. 3. Origami. 4. Paper toy-making — China.
I. Title.

TT870 .S666 2001
736'.98'0951—dc21

                                  2001047367

Manufactured in the United States of America
Dover Publications, Inc., 31 East 2nd Street, Mineola, N.Y. 11501

TO JUNIOR AMERICANS

FOREWORD

Chinese are world-renowned for their handicraft. In China, little boys and girls are taught by their elders to use their hands. Even at an early age those chubby hands with their tiny, nimble fingers, are busily engaged in making paper toys such as boats, boxes, hats, and birds, for themselves and their playmates.

This paper-folding art, as we call it in China, is done with only a single sheet of paper and your hands, without any pasting together or the use of scissors. It is the most interesting, inexpensive, and useful art for children and grownups. It gives endless joy to youngsters and also to invalids confined to the narrow limits of a home or hospital. It can be most advantageously used as therapy for patients with paralyzed hands endeavoring to regain their dexterity.

When I was a little girl my mother taught me, as her mother had taught her, how to make toys with paper. I used to spend many rainy days trying to create new objects that neither my mother nor my grandmother knew how to make. I was so proud of myself!

Of course, this was a long time ago. Now I have a little girl of my own. She loves all the things I teach her to make, especially the multicolored ones that we make together for her birthday and Christmas parties. Her little friends, and their parents, all enjoy them as much as we do. They come back time and again to get me to show them how to do the paper objects. Their eagerness and deep interest have prompted me to put my paper foldings in a book.

I hope that my American friends, especially the Junior Americans, will find great interest and enjoyment in the art of paper folding.

MAYING SOONG

CONTENTS

The contents are grouped under four convenient headings, and are not arranged chronologically.

Contents

INTRODUCTION

The different objects in this book are arranged in such a way that the simpler and easier ones are shown in the beginning of the book, while the more elaborate ones appear in the subsequent pages.

Every step is shown by a numbered figure and should be followed in accordance with the accompanying directions.

When dotted lines are shown in the figure it always means to fold the object and leave it folded, unless otherwise stated.

Folding must be accurately done so that corners and edges will meet evenly. Folds should be creased securely to make them stay in place. Usually, it is best to use the pressure of a thumb nail tip to press the fold into place.

When the directions indicate that the paper is to be folded, creased, and *unfolded* before proceeding to the next step, the creases which are indicated by a very fine line in the figure are intended to be used as a guide to keep the work accurate, or as a preparation for the next step.

A square of paper is used for making almost all of the

folded novelties described in this book. On pages x, xi and xii are shown simple methods for making accurate squares.

1. To obtain the largest square from any sized piece of paper:

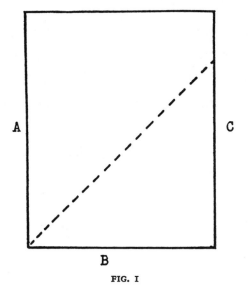

FIG. I

Fold on the dotted line by bringing line B on line A.

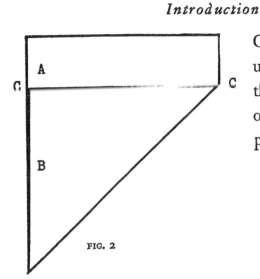

Cut on line C-C. When unfolded the square is the largest that can be obtained from this piece of paper.

FIG. 2

2. To obtain a square of any desired size:

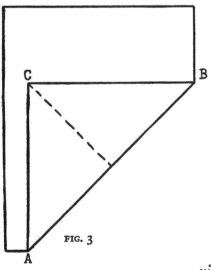

Make a diagonal fold in a piece of paper that is larger in both length and width than the desired square.

Fold again on dotted line.

FIG. 3

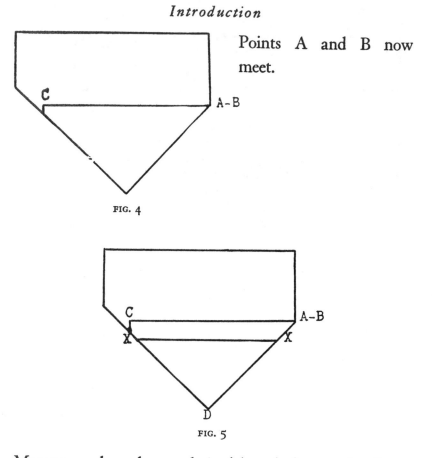

Points A and B now meet.

FIG. 4

FIG. 5

Measure and mark any desired length from point D toward A-B, and use the same length from D toward C. (Line X to X will be the length of a side of the square.)

Cut from point X to X through all folds of the paper. Unfold, and you will have a square of the desired size.

CHINESE
PAPER
FOLDING
FOR
BEGINNERS

"LOVE KNOT"

This is a good way to fold an informal letter or note. The "love knot" is specially designed to be used in schools and libraries, and in dormitory mailboxes, where notes are so often exchanged, and where envelopes are a bother.

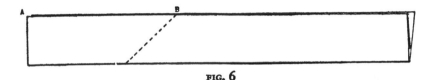

FIG. 6

Write your note on any size of writing paper. Fold the sheet into a long strip as shown in Fig. 6. Then fold on the slanted dotted line, so that line A-B will fall straight as in Fig. 7.

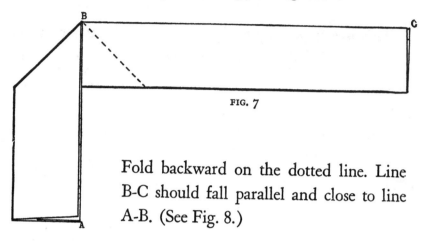

FIG. 7

Fold backward on the dotted line. Line B-C should fall parallel and close to line A-B. (See Fig. 8.)

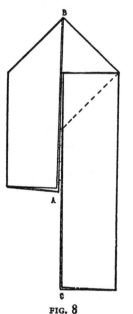

Fold backward on the dotted line.

FIG. 8

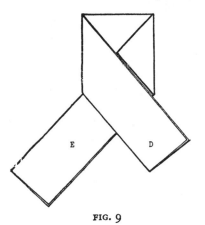

FIG. 9

Place leg D behind leg E.

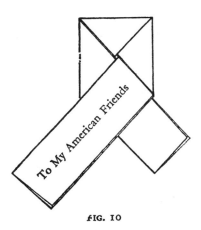

To My American Friends

FIG. 10

Finished "love knot." Write name on leg E. Now it is ready to deliver your message with love.

PAPER CUP

How to make a paper cup when you wish to have a drink and no other cup is available.

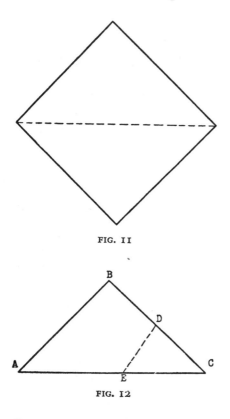

FIG. 11

Place a piece of square paper (8″ x 8″ is a good size) in the position shown in Fig. 11, and fold on the dotted line.

FIG. 12

Bring point C to line A-B so that line C-D is parallel with line A-E. (See Fig. 13.) Fold on dotted line.

Cup now in position Fig. 13.

Turn it over to the other side.

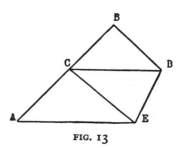

FIG. 13

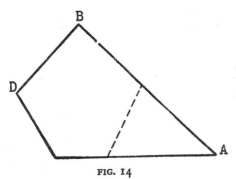

FIG. 14

Bring point A to point D. Crease on dotted line.

FIG. 15

Fold on the dotted line, bringing upper sheet of point B downward.

Turn cup over and repeat on the other side.

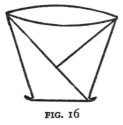

FIG. 16

Finished cup opened at the top; lower corners brought upward to keep it open.

7

DUTCH HAT

To make this hat, paper should be rectangular in shape, its length 1½ times its width. For a child to wear, use paper approximately 17" x 8½". It may also be made small enough for a doll.

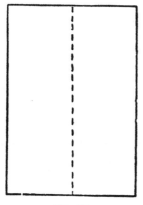

FIG. 17

Fold on the dotted line. Unfold.

Fold on the dotted line by bringing line A-B to line C-D.

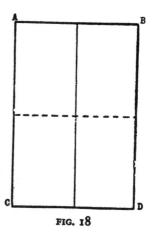

FIG. 18

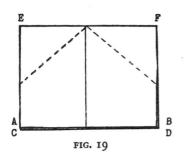

FIG. 19

Fold on the dotted lines so that point E and point F meet at the center line.

Fold on the dotted line, bringing line A-B upward.

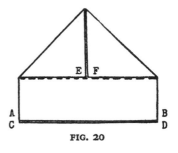

FIG. 20

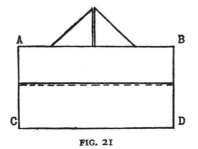

FIG. 21

Turn the hat over to the other side and bring line C-D upward, folding on the dotted line.

Finished hat, opened at the bottom and ready to be worn.

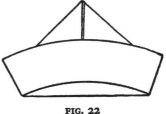

FIG. 22

9

This bird can be made nicely with writing paper. Tissue or heavy paper will not serve the purpose.

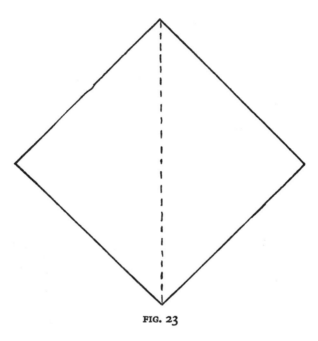

FIG. 23

Take a piece of square paper (6" x 6") and place it as in Fig. 23.

Fold on the dotted line. Crease, and unfold.

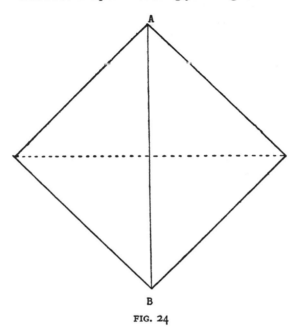

FIG. 24

Bring point A to point B and fold on the dotted line.

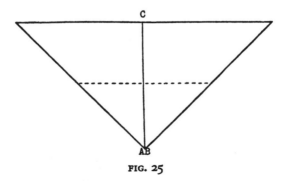

FIG. 25

Bring point AB to point C and fold on the dotted line.

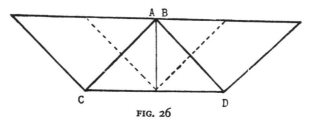

FIG. 26

Fold on dotted lines by bringing point D to AB and point C to AB.

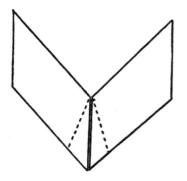

FIG. 27

Fold on the dotted lines. Crease, and unfold.

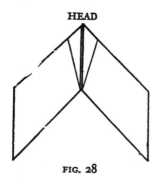

HEAD

FIG. 28

Turn the bird upside down. Push up the head through the center. Crease well.

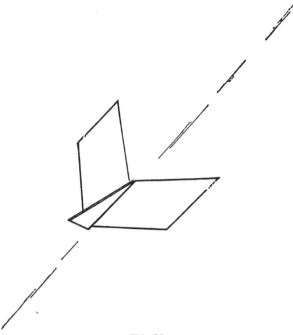

FIG. 29

Finished bird that will fly when thrown from the fingers. To fly this bird, hold its head between your index and middle finger. Lift your hand up high and throw the bird off with a little swing. It can fly gracefully for some distance.

DUSTPAN

Little girls can use a miniature dustpan when they are playing house.

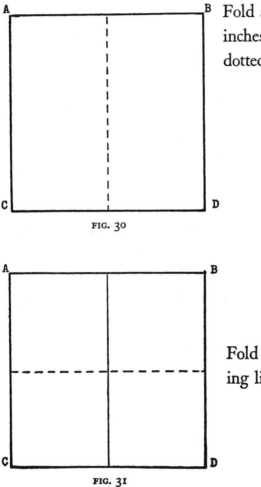

Fold a square of paper, 8 inches or smaller, on the dotted line. Unfold.

FIG. 30

Fold on dotted line, bringing line A-B to line C-D

FIG. 31

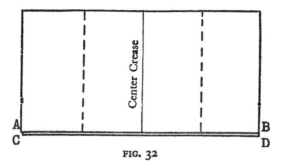

FIG. 32

Fold on the dotted lines, bringing points AC and BD together at the center crease.

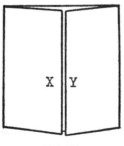

FIG. 33

Folded paper now looks as in Fig. 33.

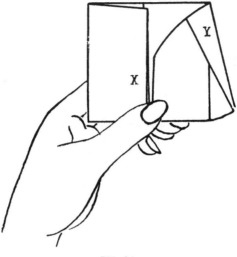

FIG. 34

Study Fig. 34 before proceeding.

Slip left thumb inside Y, and holding underside firmly in place with thumb, pull upperside all of the way out to the right. Crease on the diagonal lines at the top. (See Fig. 35.) Repeat with X.

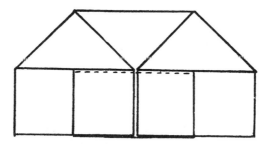

FIG. 35

Fold on the dotted line upward.

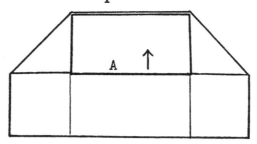

FIG. 36

Open dustpan by pushing line A up.

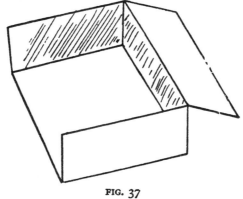

FIG. 37

Finished dustpan.

PINWHEEL

Children always love pinwheels. It's fun to be able to make them yourself.

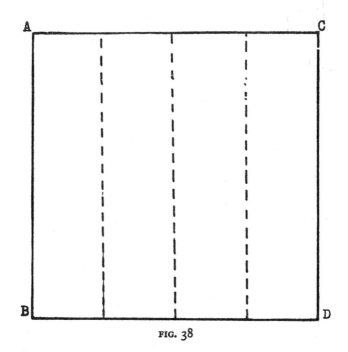

FIG. 38

Fold a square approximately 8½″ down the middle Crease. Unfold.

Bring lines A-B and C-D to center crease line. Fold.

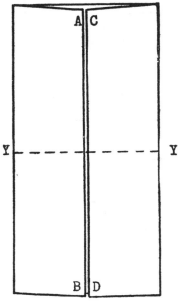

FIG. 39

Fold on the dotted line Y-Y. Crease. Unfold.

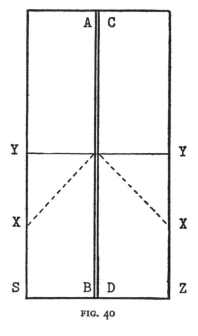

FIG. 40

Pick up lower corner D and lift upward to right, matching edge (line C-D) with creased line Y. Fold across diagonal dotted line.

Repeat with lower corner B, lifting it upward toward left and folding.

Fold underside from X to X and crease flat.

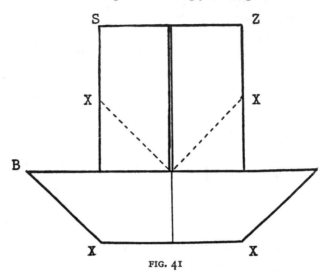

FIG. 41

Pinwheel now looks like Fig. 41. Turn it upside down and repeat steps in Fig. 40.

When completed model will look as in Fig. 42.

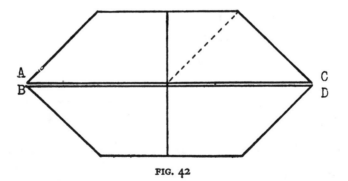

FIG. 42

Bring point C upward by folding on the dotted line.

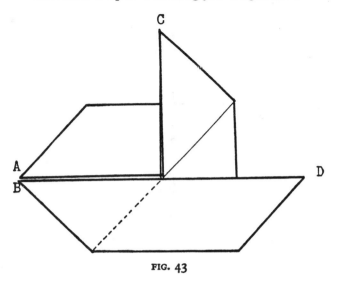

FIG. 43

Fold on the dotted line by bringing point B downward

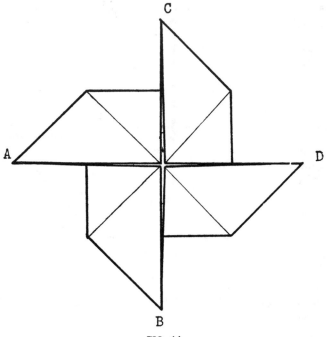

C

A   D

B

FIG. 44

Folded pinwheel.

Cut two small ½″ squares. Paste one over the center to catch the corners together. Stick a pin through the center of the pinwheel, then through the center of the second small square, and then push it firmly into a stick.

Pull the flaps of the pinwheel open, and it is ready for a whirl in the breeze.

SMALL BOX

Boxes are always useful for children's collections. Heavy writing or wrapping paper will be most suitable to make the box.

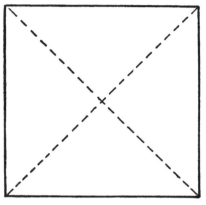

FIG. 45

Fold a square of paper diagonally on the dotted lines. Crease. Unfold.

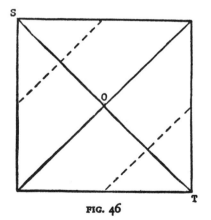

FIG. 46

Fold and crease on the dotted lines by bringing corners S and T to center O. Unfold.

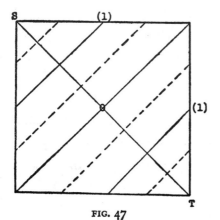

FIG. 47

Bring point S to crease (1), then fold by rolling over again and again on the dotted lines until fold meets center O.

Repeat with point T.

When this step is finished it should look like Fig. 48.

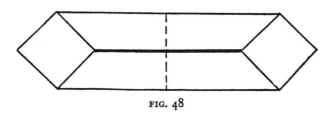

FIG. 48

Fold to the back at dotted line.

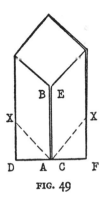

FIG. 49

Fold on the dotted lines by bringing line A-B on line A-D, and line C-E on line C-F, creasing on diagonal line. Then crease across points X.

When finished turn Fig. 49 over and place it in position Fig. 50.

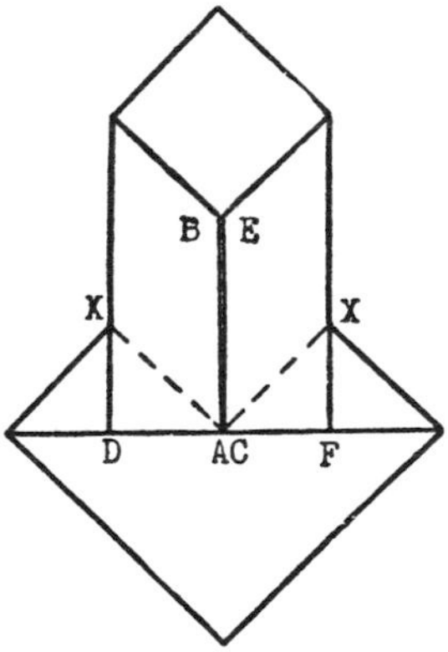

FIG. 50

Repeat steps in Fig. 49 to Fig. 50.

Fold upper section on dotted lines so that points P meet at center line.

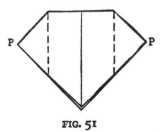

FIG. 51

25

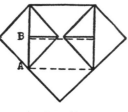

FIG. 52

First fold at dotted line A, then turn over again at dotted line B.

When the above is done, turn Fig. 52 over and repeat steps in Fig. 51 and Fig. 52 on other side.

FIG. 53

Open box by pulling flaps A and B apart with thumbs and index fingers while supporting bottom of box with other fingers.

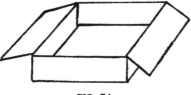

FIG. 54

Finished box.

ROW BOAT

This row boat made of waxed paper, cellophane, or other waterproof paper will float in water for a long time.

Matchsticks and toothpicks can be used in the smaller boats for seats and oars, and to make them look lifelike.

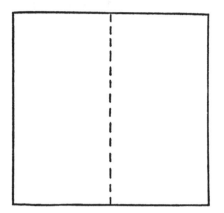

FIG. 55

Fold a square in half and crease.

Unfold.

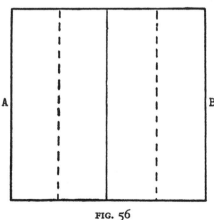

FIG. 56

Bring lines A and B to center fold and crease.

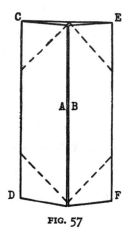

FIG. 57

Fold on diagonal dotted lines, bringing points C, D, E and F to the center line and crease.

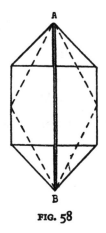

FIG. 58

Fold on dotted lines.

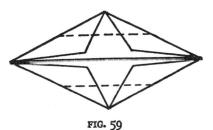

FIG. 59

Fold again on dotted lines.

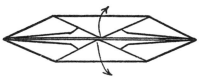

FIG. 60

Turn boat inside out, holding folds carefully to prevent tearing.

FIG. 61

Finished boat, ready for the bathtub sailor.

NAVY CAP

This hat can be made of colored gift-wrapping paper. Children enjoy making their own hats and it adds fun to parties.

Paper should be rectangular in shape, its length 1½ times its width. For a child's hat, use paper approximately 21″ x 14″.

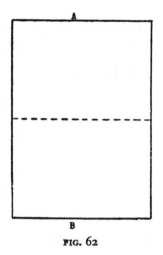

FIG. 62

Fold paper on the dotted line, bringing line A to B.

Fold on lines 1 and 2, crease and unfold.

Fold on the diagonal dotted lines.

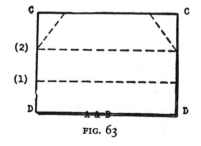

FIG. 63

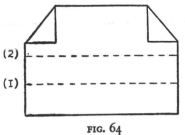

(2)

(1)

FIG. 64

Fold the upper sheet on the dotted lines, folding first on line (1), then rolling over again to crease on line (2). When done, turn Fig. 64 over.

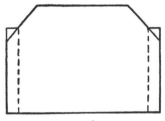

FIG. 65

Fold on the dotted lines. Crease well.

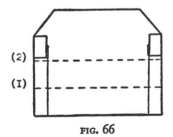

(2)

(1)

FIG. 66

Fold this side on lines (1) and (2), as in Fig. 64. When completed, tuck ends at top securely into each end of the folded band to hold it in place.

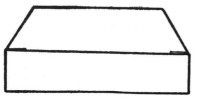

Open the hat at the bottom.

FIG. 67

FIG. 68

Completed hat, ready to wear.

PAPER BALL

Paper balls make attractive Christmas tree ornaments when made of shiny, colored papers, or with cellophane. They also can be used as party favors and decorations.

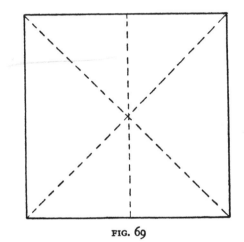

FIG. 69

Take a square of paper, fold, and crease on the dotted lines. Unfold.

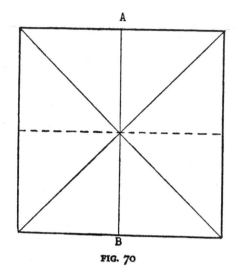

FIG. 70

Fold on the dotted line, bringing A to B.

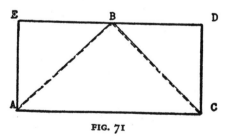

FIG. 71

Fold on the dotted lines by pushing triangles C B D, and A B E *into* triangle A B C. Hold paper in hand as illustrated in Fig. 72.

34

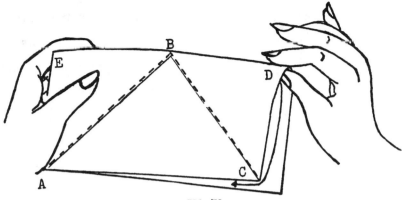

FIG. 72

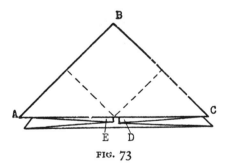

FIG. 73

Fold upper sheet on the dotted lines, bringing point A and point C to point B.

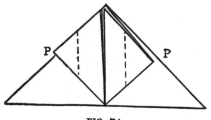

FIG. 74

Fold again on the dotted lines, bringing points P of the upper sheet to the center.

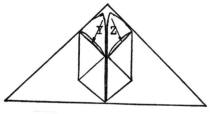

FIG. 75

Tuck flaps Y and Z into the two pockets shown by the arrows until they are even and smooth. Crease.

These flaps will have to be pushed into the pockets.

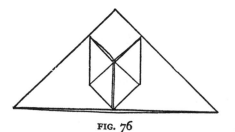

FIG. 76

Turn Fig. 76 over and repeat steps in Figs. 73, 74 and 75.

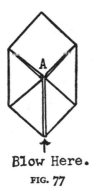

Blow Here.

FIG. 77

Fill the ball with air by blowing into the small hole in the end.

Hold the ball by putting the index fingers of both hands against corners A and touching the outer crease with thumbs and fingers. This will prevent the ball from unfolding as it expands.

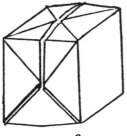

FIG. 78

Finished ball.

CHINESE KNIGHT'S HELMET

The knight's helmet will add another hat to the variety that children love to wear when playing. It is not difficult to fold, but looks quite fancy when finished. If you wish a hat in two colors, use two different-colored squares, placed on top of each other, and treat them as a single square.

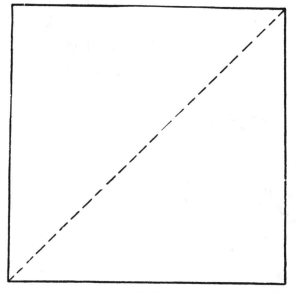

FIG. 79

Fold a piece of square paper diagonally on the dotted line
For a child's hat, use paper approximately 22″ square.

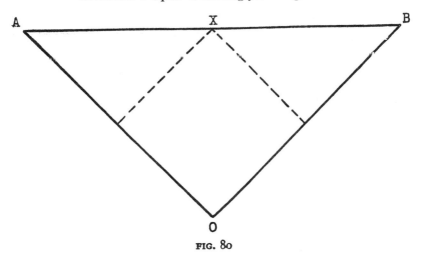

FIG. 80

Place the paper in position as in Fig. 80. Fold on the dotted lines, bringing points A and B to point O.

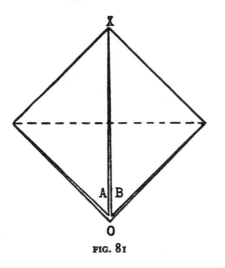

FIG. 81

Bring A and B to point X. Crease on dotted line. Point O stays in position.

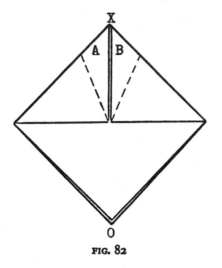

FIG. 82

Turn points A and B outward, folding on the dotted lines of Fig. 82 to make Fig. 83.

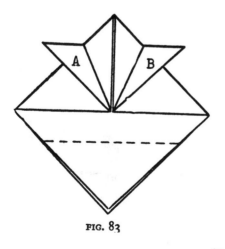

FIG. 83

Fold top sheet upward on dotted line.

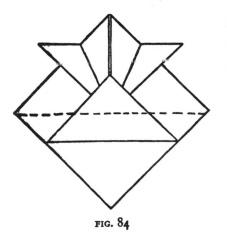

FIG. 84

Fold upper sheet upward again on dotted line. Turn hat (Fig. 84) over to other side.

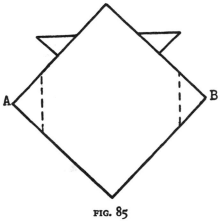

FIG. 85

Fold points A and B toward center on dotted lines.

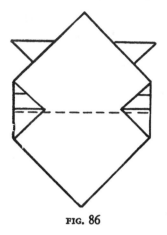

FIG. 86

Fold upward on dotted line. When finished turn Fig. 86 over.

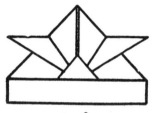

FIG. 87

Open hat at bottom.

FIG. 88

Completed Chinese knight's helmet.

CHINESE FISHING BOAT

Fishing boat with awnings. Be sure to crease each fold firmly so that the finished boat will turn inside out easily. If waterproofed paper is used, this boat will float.

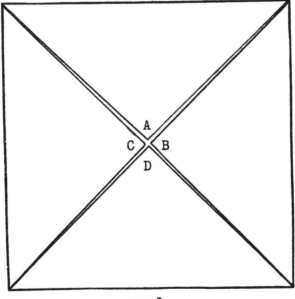

FIG. 89

Follow directions for Figs. 115 and 116 to get illustration, Fig. 89.

Do not turn figure over as stated in directions for Fig. 116

43

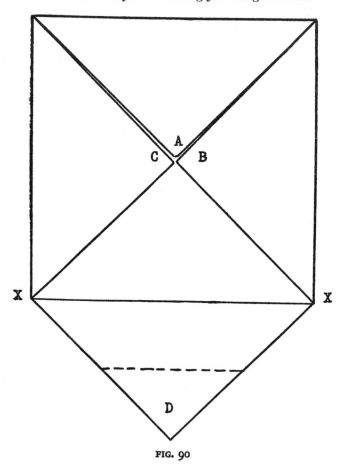

FIG. 90

Fold on the dotted line, bringing point D to line X-X.
Fold over again on line X-X.

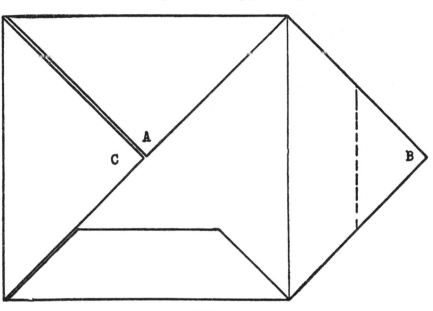

FIG. 91

Repeat directions in Fig. 90 for points A, B and C. When all four sides are done, you should have Fig. 92.

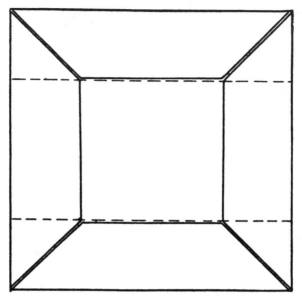

FIG. 92

Fold toward the back, on the dotted lines.

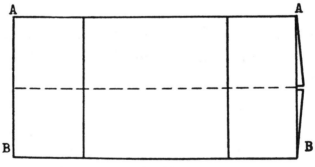

FIG. 93

Place paper in position shown in Fig. 93.

Fold on the dotted line, bringing line A-A to line B-B

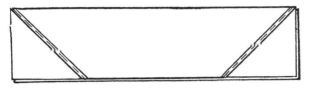

FIG. 94

The boat now looks as in Fig. 94. Fold the upper layer on the dotted lines and crease.

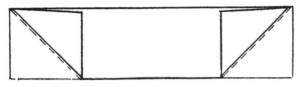

FIG. 95

Fold the lower layer toward the back on the dotted lines.

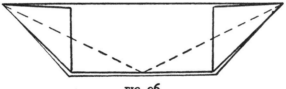

FIG. 96

Fold the upper layer on the dotted lines.

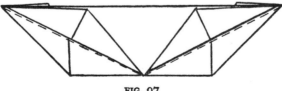

FIG. 97

Fold the lower layer toward the back on the dotted lines.

47

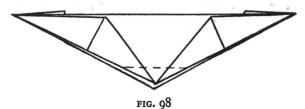

FIG. 98

Fold the top layer upward and the lower layer backward on dotted line.

FIG. 99

Boat is now in position, Fig. 99.

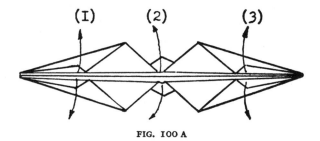

FIG. 100 A

Place boat in floating position. Turn boat inside out carefully, holding all folds tightly in place to prevent loosening. You can do it in three steps (1), (2), and (3), respectively, as shown by the arrows. Study holding in Fig. 100 B.

48

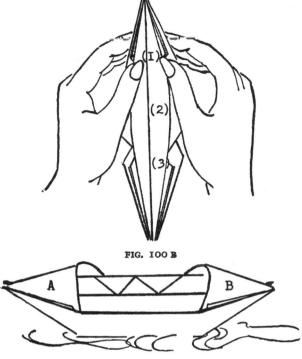

FIG. 100 B

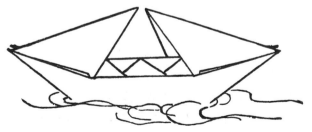

FIG. 101 A

View of finished boat on a sunny day. For rainy weather, pull out under layer of A and B, Fig. 101 A.

FIG. 101 B

View of finished boat on a rainy day.

49

"OLD SCHOLAR" HAT

Here is still another hat to add to the play and party collection. For a child to wear, use paper approximately 20″ square.

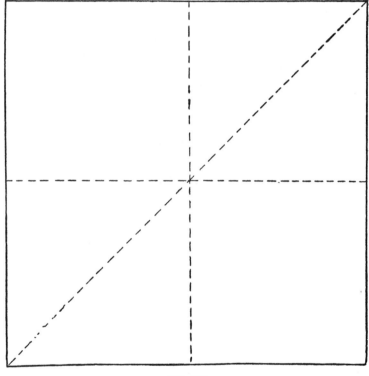

FIG. 102

Fold a square on the dotted lines as in Fig. 102. Crease. Unfold.

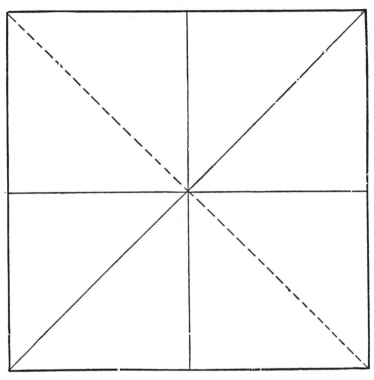

FIG. 103

Fold on the dotted line.

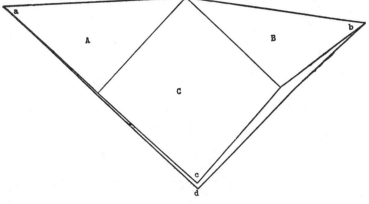

FIG. 104

Bring points b and a *between* points c and d by pushing triangle B and triangle A into square C.

Folds will fall easily on previously formed creases.

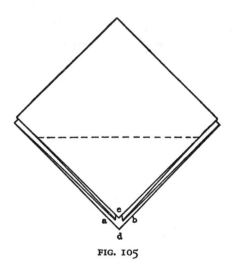

FIG. 105

Bring point c up, folding on dotted line. (Upper sheet only.)

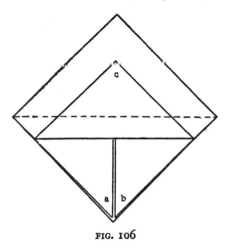

FIG. 106

Fold again on dotted line.

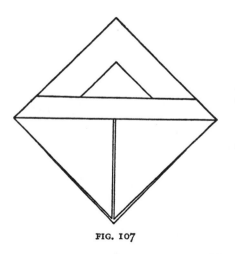

FIG. 107

Hat now in position Fig. 107. Turn it over on the other side.

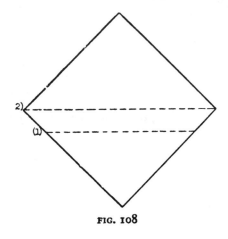

Fold upper sheet only on the dotted lines (1) and (2), repeating same folding as in Fig. 105 and Fig. 106.

FIG. 108

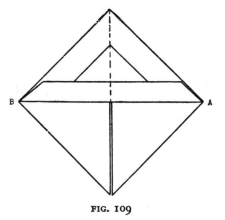

Fold on dotted line, bringing point A to point B.

Repeat same on back.

FIG. 109

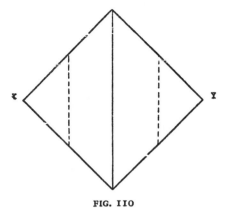

FIG. 110

Fold upper layer on dotted lines so that points X and Y will meet on the center line.

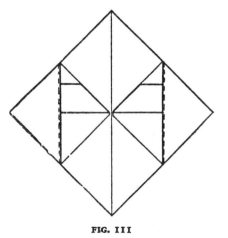

FIG. 111

Repeat, folding lower layer toward back on the dotted lines.

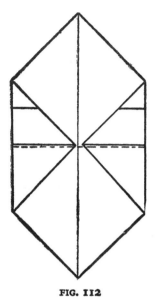

FIG. 112

Fold on the dotted line, bringing the upper layer toward the front, the lower layer toward the back.

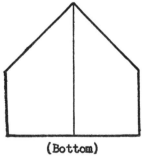

(Bottom)

FIG. 113

Open the hat by pulling apart gently at the bottom of the flaps that were folded upward in Fig. 112.

Ease the crown of the hat into place from the inside.

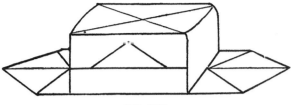

FIG. 114

Completed Ming Dynasty officer's hat for a would-be officer.

FOOTSTOOL

Little girls can make a footstool for their own doll house furniture.

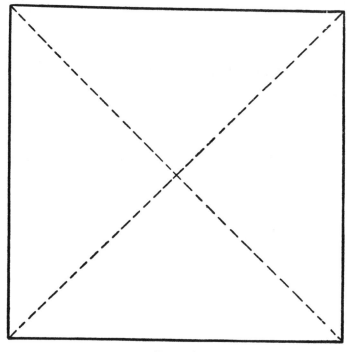

FIG. 115

Use a square piece of paper (any size desired). Fold and crease on the dotted lines.

Unfold.

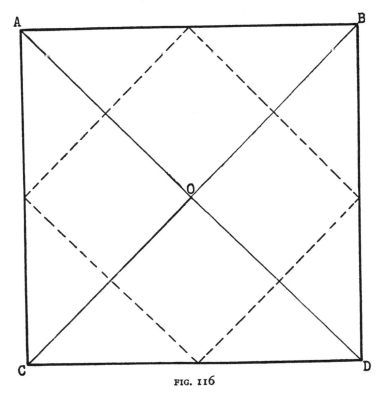

FIG. 116

Bring points A, B, C and D to center point O. Crease on dotted lines.

When finished turn Fig. 116 over to the other side.

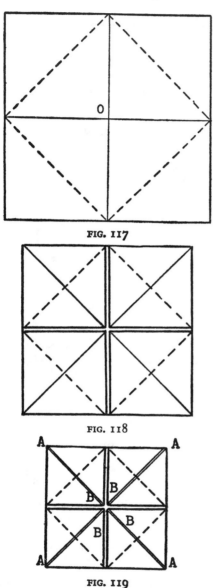

FIG. 117

Again bring corners to center O and crease on the dotted lines.

When done, turn paper over to the other side.

FIG. 118

Fold on the dotted lines, bringing corners to center again, and crease.

Turn to the other side.

FIG. 119

Open each corner square by bringing point B to point A (opening and spreading upper layer outward, as in Fig. 120).

Crease on the dotted lines.

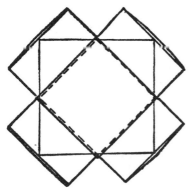

FIG. 120

Fold toward the back on the dotted lines.

Crease firmly, pressing tightly before releasing.

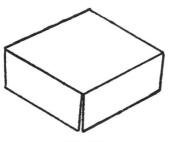

FIG. 121

Release edges and adjust legs in place, and you have a footstool.

CHAIR

Another piece of furniture for a doll house.

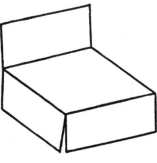

FIG. 122

Repeat the directions for the footstool, Figs. 115, 116, 117, 118, 119 and 120.

When following directions for Fig. 120, fold three sides backward and one side forward.

This will give the chair a back.

DISPOSABLE COASTER

This coaster can be made with colored paper to fit in with any color scheme for party table decorations. Its points come up around the base of the glass like petals, which makes it very attractive.

Use a seven-inch square of paper for an ordinary eight-ounce glass coaster.

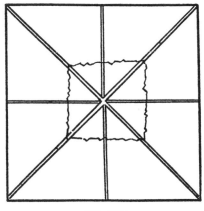

FIG. 123

Follow directions in Figs. 115, 116 and 117 to get illustration Fig. 123. (Do not turn Fig. 117 over.)

Fasten the corners in the center with a small piece of Scotch tape. Coaster is now in position shown in Fig. 123.

Turn paper over to the other side.

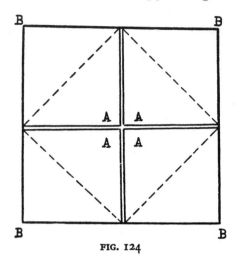

FIG. 124

Fold and crease on dotted lines by bringing points A to points B.

FIG. 125

Finished coaster.

Adjust the petals so they stand up gracefully.

POKE BONNET

Little girls always look attractive in poke bonnets. Here is a model you can make in a few minutes.

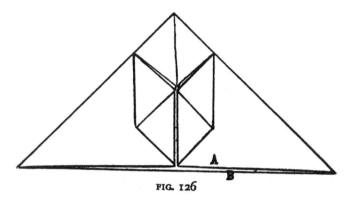

FIG. 126

Use a 24-inch square of pastel crepe paper (other paper can also be used) for a child's bonnet.

Follow Figs. 69, 70, 71, 72, 73, 74 and 75 to get the illustration Fig. 126.

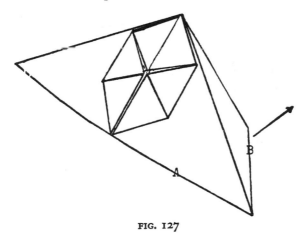

To open, hold Fig. 127 with left fingers. Pull carefully outward with right fingers at point B, then insert right fingers inside bonnet and push outward until crown is completely opened at back.

When finished it should look like Fig. 128.

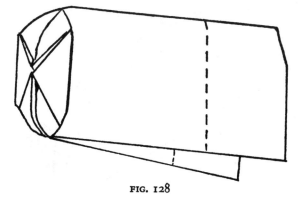

FIG. 128

Fold on dotted line to make a cuff for the bonnet.

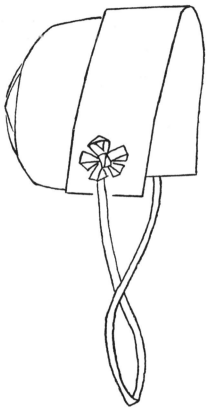

FIG. 129

Decorate the finished bonnet with contrasting colored bows and streamers of crepe paper.

If paper is cut with the grain it will tie in bows without stretching.

It will look even nicer if you decorate the bonnet with real ribbons.

TENT

The amateur general can lay out a camp for his army of tin soldiers. Row on row of gleaming white tents lend importance to his battles.

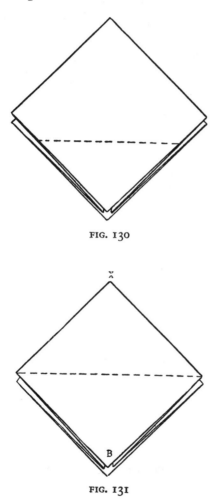

FIG. 130

FIG. 131

Use a 10-inch square piece of paper, or larger.

Follow Figs. 102, 103 and 104 to get the illustration Fig. 130.

Fold top sheet only on the dotted line and crease.

When finished turn Fig. 130 over to the other side.

Fold and crease on the dotted line by bringing point B to point X.

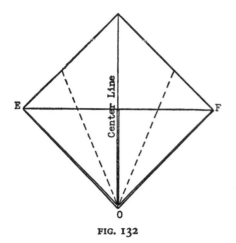

FIG. 132

Bring line E-O and line F-O of upper sheet to center line. Crease on dotted lines.

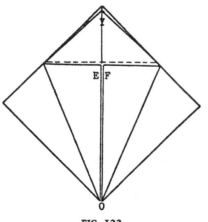

FIG. 133

Fold upper sheet only on the dotted line, bringing corner Y downward.

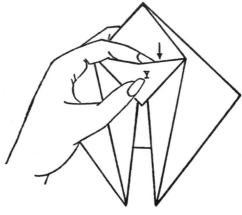

FIG. 134

To open, hold firmly with left thumb on flap Y, and index finger inside pocket shown by arrow.

Insert right fingers in tent and push carefully until completely opened.

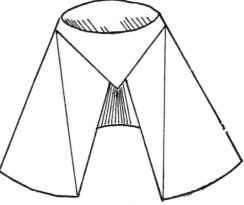

FIG. 135

Completed tent.

EASTER SURPRISE BUNNY

The bunny will add an extra bit of delight to an Easter party. You can even push jelly beans into him through his mouth, if you do it carefully.

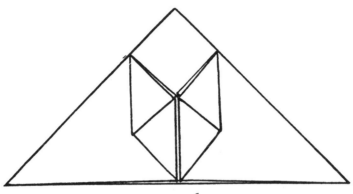

FIG. 136

Use a square piece of paper of any desired size.

Follow the directions in Figs. 69, 70, 71, 72, 73, 74 and 75 to get the illustration in Fig. 136.

Turn Fig. 136 to the other side.

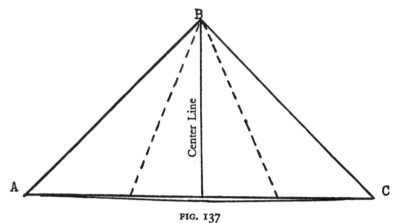

FIG. 137

Bring line A-B and line C-B to center line, and crease on dotted lines.

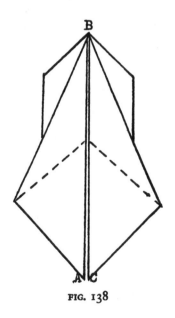

FIG. 138

Fold and crease on the dotted lines.

74

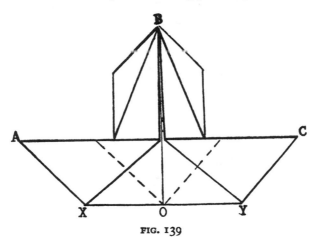

Fold and crease on the dotted lines by bringing line X-O and line Y-O to center line O-B.

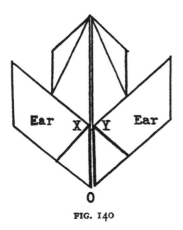

FIG. 140

Open bunny by placing index finger of left hand on point X-Y. Lift ears up and hold them each side of index finger, with thumb and first finger.

Blow at point O.

FIG. 141

Finished bunny.

(Draw eyes and whiskers with pencil, if you wish.)

STEAMBOATS

These boats won't float—but the captains and crews of little boys' parties will approve the paper Navy.

Use an 8-inch square of paper (preferably gray color) for the first boat and smaller size paper for the boats in the distance.

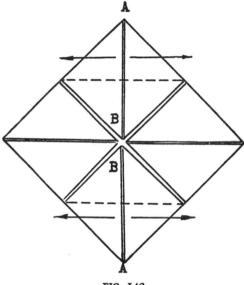

FIG. 142

Follow Figs. 115, 116, 117 and 118 to get illustration, Fig. 142.

Open upper and lower squares by bringing points B to points A (opening and spreading upper layers outward).

77

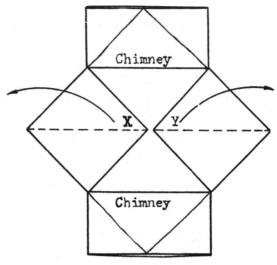

FIG. 143

To open steamboat, bring points X and Y upward and outward—and at the same time bringing the chimneys together.

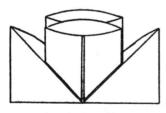

FIG. 144

Finished steamboats.

WINGED HAT

Another hat to add to the variety for parties.

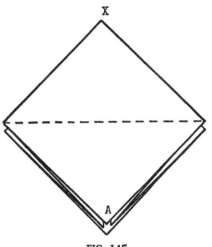

FIG. 145

Use a 24-inch square for a child's hat.

Follow directions for Figs. 102, 103 and 104 to get illustration Fig. 145.

Bring point A to point X and crease on the dotted line.

Turn to other side and repeat.

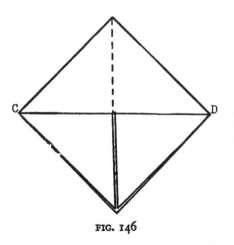

FIG. 146

Fold on the dotted line, bringing point C to point D.

Turn to the other side and repeat.

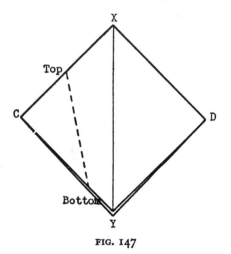

FIG. 147

Fold upper layer on the dotted line. The top of the dotted line is halfway between C-X; the bottom is one third of the distance between C-Y.

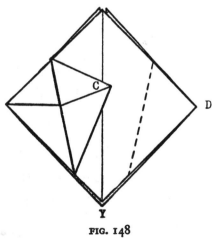

FIG. 148

Fold on the dotted line. Note that corners C and D overlap each other.

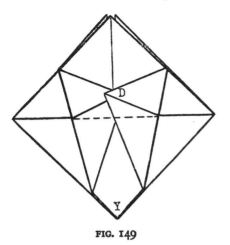

FIG. 149

Fold on the dotted line upward.

Crease.

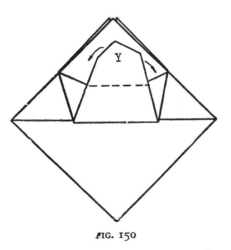

FIG. 150

Fold on the dotted line, tucking flap Y behind points C and D. (Figs. 148 and 149.)

Turn to the other side and repeat directions for Figs. 147, 148, 149 and 150.

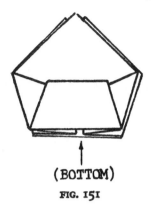

Open hat at the bottom. (Be careful not to undo any foldings.)

(BOTTOM)

FIG. 151

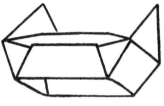

FIG. 152

Finished winged hat.

CANDY AND PLACE CARD
BASKET

This candy basket can be made very attractive with colored papers to fit into any party scheme. A name can be written on each of these baskets as they are being folded so that they can also serve as place cards.

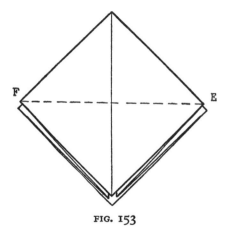

FIG. 153

Use an 8″ square of paper and follow the directions for Figs. 102, 103 and 104 to get illustration Fig. 153.

Fold all layers together on the dotted lines. Crease and unfold.

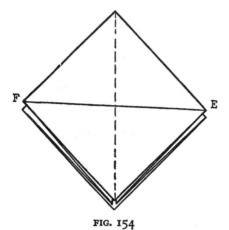

FIG. 154

Bring point E (top layer only) to the left on F.

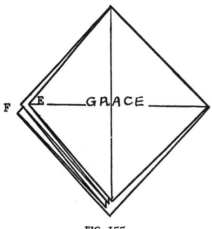

FIG. 155

Add name, centering it by using creased guide lines.

Return point E to its former position (as in Fig. 153).

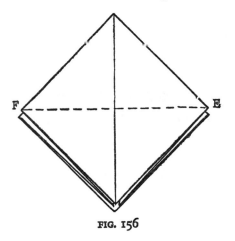

FIG. 156

Fold (top sheet only) on the dotted line.

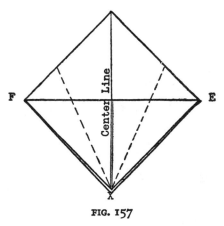

FIG. 157

Bring lines X-F and X-F (top layer only) to center line.

Fold on the dotted lines.

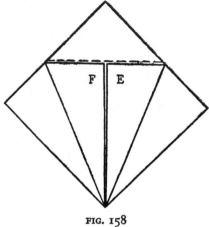

FIG. 158

Fold downward on the dotted line, then turn Fig. 158 to other side and repeat directions for Figs. 156, 157 and 158.

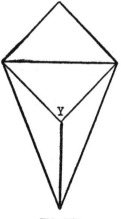

FIG. 159

To open, hold both sides at flap Y, and pull apart.

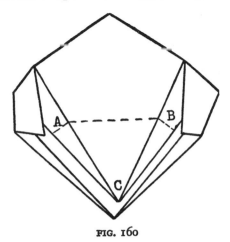

FIG. 160

Fold on the dotted line, pushing triangle A B C to the inside.

Repeat the above directions on the other side.

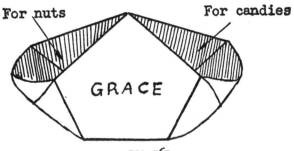

FIG. 161

Finished candy and place card basket.

LIGHTHOUSE BOOKMARK

Every reader likes to have a nice bookmark. Here is one that you can make. Write your favorite motto on it.

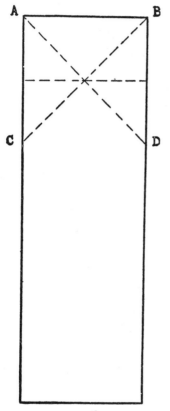

FIG. 162

Cut a piece of paper 8 inches long and 2½ inches wide.

Fold on the dotted lines by bringing line A-B to line B-D, crease and unfold: line A-B to line A-C, crease and unfold: line A-B to line C-D, crease and unfold.

To get Fig. 163, follow directions for Figs. 69, 70, 71 and 72.

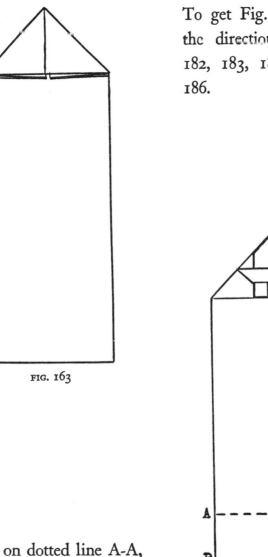

FIG. 163

To get Fig. 164, follow the directions for Figs. 182, 183, 184, 185 and 186.

FIG. 164

Fold on dotted line A-A, about one inch from base.

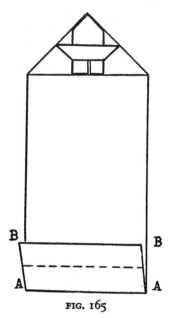

FIG. 165

Fold on the dotted line, bringing line B-B to line A-A.

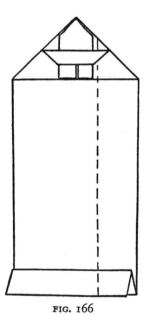

FIG. 166

Fold backward on the dotted line, approximately one-third of the width.

Turn paper over to the other side.

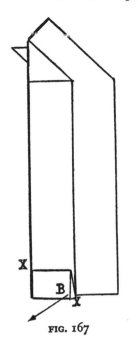

Pull corner B down toward the left, creasing on a line from points X to X.

FIG. 167

Cut on dotted line C-X, then fold at the lengthwise dotted line and pull lower corner down, as in Fig. 167, but toward the right side, and cut.

When finished, turn Fig. 168 over.

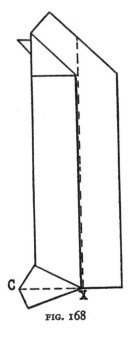

FIG. 168

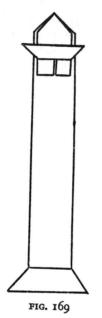

The lighthouse bookmark
is ready for your favorite
proverb or motto.

FIG. 169

MONKEY

This is another toy that you can make yourself and have lots of fun.

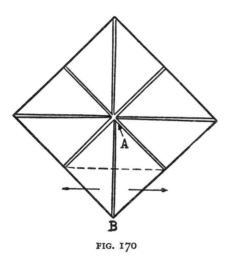

FIG. 170

To get Fig. 170, follow the directions for Figs. 115, 116, 117 and 118.

Bring point A to point B by opening square and folding on dotted line.

Pull corner Y all the way up and out to the right. This will include unfolding all of the right side on the back as well.

Paper now in position as illustrated in Fig. 172.

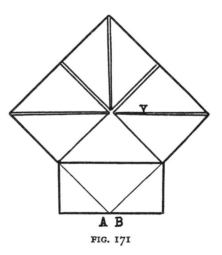

FIG. 171

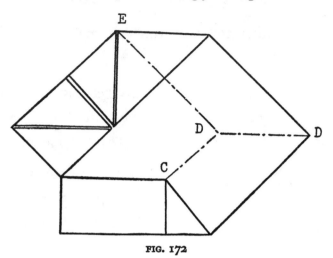

FIG. 172

Fold backward on dotted line C-D; almost at the same time fold backward on dotted line E-DD.

Repeat directions for Fig. 171 and Fig. 172 to left side of paper.

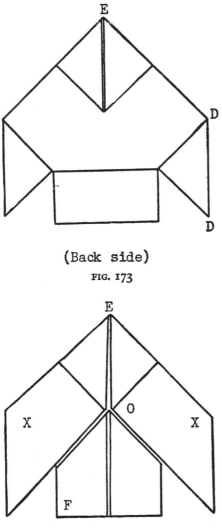

It now appears as illustrated in Fig. 173.

Turn it over to the other side (front side).

(Back side)

FIG. 173

(Front side)

FIG. 174

Place index finger of left hand against point O, and bring parts X toward each other with thumb and first finger. (See Fig. 175.)

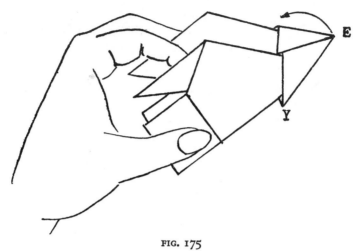

FIG. 175

It is being held in left hand as shown in Fig. 175. Then, with right index finger push frontward on E. At same time use right thumb to bring Y upward.

Note position of Y and E in Fig. 176.

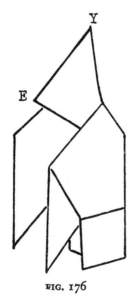

FIG. 176

Side view of finished monkey. Eyes and mouth may be added with pencil. It can stand by itself.

The bird is one of the most amusing objects. Its wings can be made to flap.

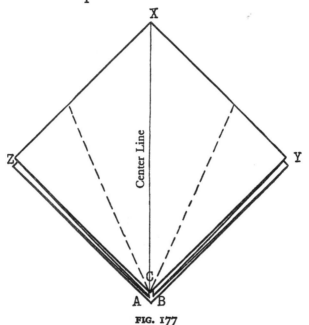

FIG. 177

Use a square piece of paper, any size desired.

Follow the directions for Figs. 102, 103 and 104 to get illustration in Fig. 177.

Bring line C-Z and C-Y to center line. Crease on the dotted lines. Unfold.

Turn Fig. 177 over to the other side and repeat the above directions.

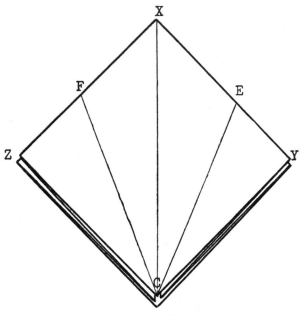

FIG. 178

Push triangle C Y E inside triangle C E X and fold on the creased line C-E.

Push triangle C Z F inside triangle C F X and fold on the creased line C-F.

Turn it over to the other side and repeat the above directions.

When finished on both sides, model appears as illustrated in Fig. 179.

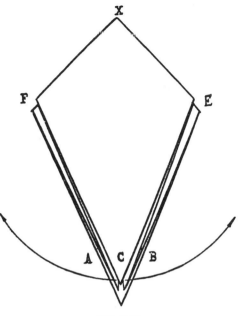

FIG. 179

Bring point B out and up, reversing the crease down its center as it is being pulled out. Bring it up into position at an angle as indicated in Fig. 180. Before creasing it into position, examine edges inside. They must be flat and smooth the whole length of the crease, especially at the center of the bird.

Repeat the above directions with point A.

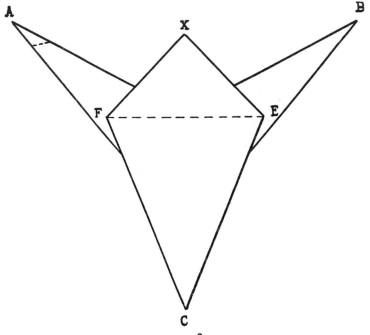

FIG. 180

The head of the bird is made by reversing the crease at the tip of point A and folding on the dotted line indicated there.

The wings are brought into position by bringing point C upward and creasing on the dotted line E-F. Repeat same directions on the reverse side.

FIG. 181

Finished bird.

Hold it in position as in Fig. 181. Pull and push the tail in and out to make the wings flap.

CHINESE PAGODA BOOKMARK

You will need nine squares to make this intricate bookmark. It is especially attractive when made from glossy paper of different colors.

Each flight is made separately, and inserted one into the other according to size.

Perfect cutting of the squares, and careful folding, is necessary to make this model successfully. It is not difficult, but the work must be exact.

The squares are cut to size as follows: $3\frac{1}{2}''$; $3\frac{1}{4}''$; $3''$; $2\frac{3}{4}''$; $2\frac{1}{2}''$; $2\frac{1}{4}''$; $2''$; $1\frac{3}{4}''$ and $1\frac{1}{2}''$. It will be noted that they graduate from $3\frac{1}{2}''$ to $1\frac{1}{2}''$ with $\frac{1}{4}''$ difference in size between each square.

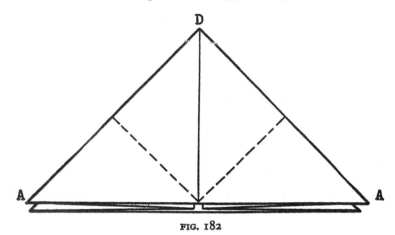

FIG. 182

Begin with the 3½" square which will become the bottom flight.

To get Fig. 182, follow directions for Figs. 69, 70, 71 and 72.

Bring points A to point D. Crease on the dotted lines.

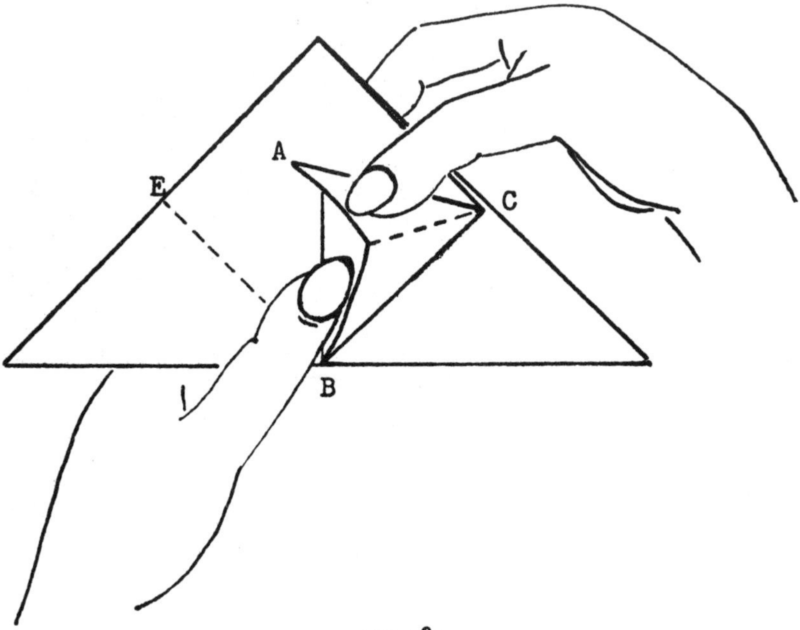

FIG. 183

Hold paper in position Fig. 183. (Put left thumb inside triangle A B C.) Use right thumb to push line C-A down until triangle A B C opens into a square.

Reverse your hand position and repeat same directions to the left side of Fig. 183.

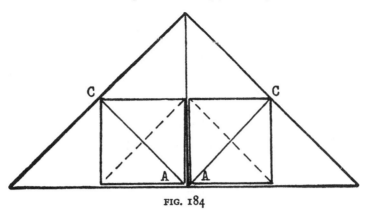

FIG. 184

Fold on dotted lines by bringing points A to points C.

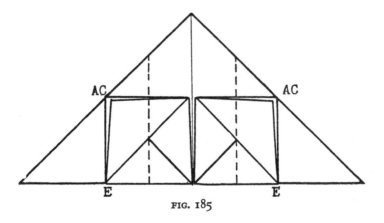

FIG. 185

It is now in position illustrated in Fig. 185.

Fold top layer toward back on dotted lines, turning edges E-AC to inside. Crease on each side.

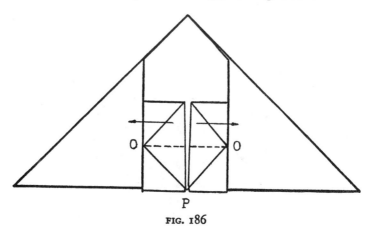

FIG. 186

Open the lines apart to left and right as indicated by the arrows in Fig. 186, and at the same time bring point P upward and fold across line O-O.

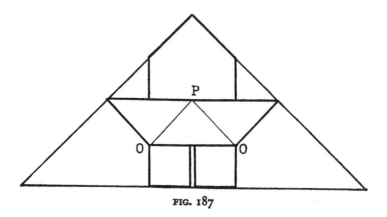

FIG. 187

Turn it (Fig. 187) over to other side and repeat directions for Figs. 182, 183, 184, 185 and 186.

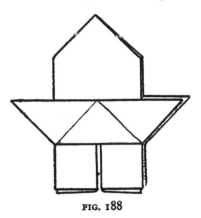

FIG. 188

Finished first flight (Fig. 188).

Repeat the above directions from Fig. 182 to Fig. 187 on the other eight flights.

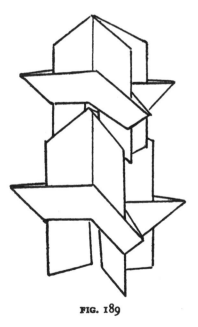

FIG. 189

Attach the flights together by slipping the two legs of the smaller flight into the grooves of the next larger crown.

Push into place until the peak of the crown slides out of sight.

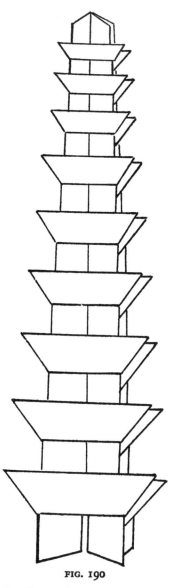

FIG. 190

Finished pagoda bookmark.

FLOWERED CANDY BOX

This is an attractive and practical box which can be made with a single sheet of paper. It may serve as an individual candy box on tables at Christmas parties, etc.

A rectangular piece of paper consisting of two equal squares is used to make this box. 4″ x 8″ is a good size for the above purpose.

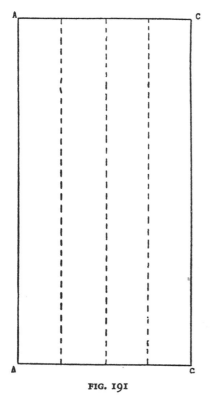

Fold on the center dotted line and crease. Unfold, then bring lines A-A and C-C to center crease, and fold.

FIG. 191

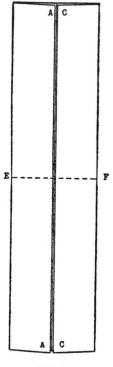

FIG. 192

Fold toward the back, on dotted line E-F.

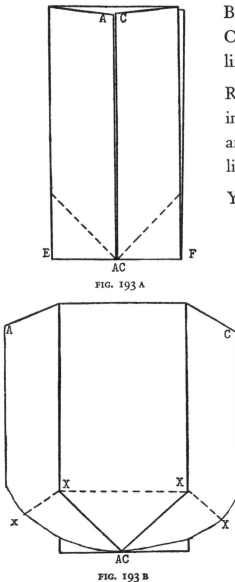

Bring line C-C on line C-F by creasing on dotted line.

Repeat on left side, bringing line A-A on line A-E, and creasing on dotted line.

You will have Fig. 193 B.

FIG. 193 A

Then crease on the dotted line X-X.

When this step is finished turn it over and repeat the directions for Figs. 193 A and 193 B on the other side.

FIG. 193 B

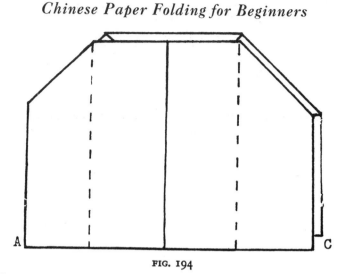

FIG. 194

Fold on the dotted lines, bringing points **A and C** to center line.

Turn it over and repeat the above directions to the other side.

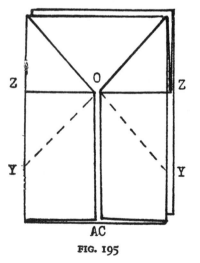

FIG. 195

Bring line C-O to line O-Z, and crease on dotted line.

Bring A-O to line O-Z, and crease on dotted line.

Then crease across Y to Y.

Turn to the other side and repeat the above directions.

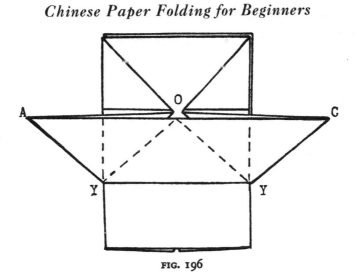

FIG. 196

Open triangle O Y A into a square. (See Fig. 197.)

FIG. 197

Review the position of Y in Fig. 196. Open the right triangle O Y C into a square in the same way.

Then turn the model over and repeat directions for Fig. 196 and Fig. 197 to the other side.

When this step is finished, it should look as in Fig. 198.

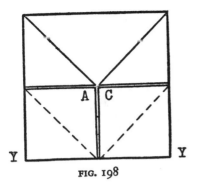

FIG. 198

Bring points A and C to points Y and crease on dotted lines.

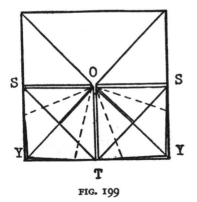

FIG. 199

Fold on the dotted lines by bringing lines O-T and O-S to the center line O-Y.

Repeat this operation on left side.

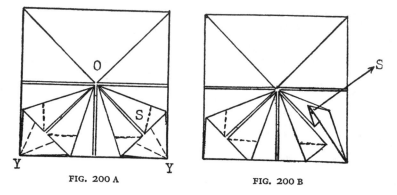

FIG. 200 A   FIG. 200 B

Fold corner S on the dotted line (200 A), pushing it upward and outward when folding.

Study corner S in Fig. 200 B and fold the other three corners in the same way.

When finished, turn over and repeat directions for Figs. 198, 199 and 200, on the other side.

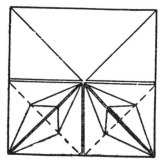

FIG. 201

Fold upper section toward back on the dotted lines. Turn to the other side and repeat.

FIG. 202

Pull little points out into position (Fig. 202).

Fold upper section downward on the dotted line.

Repeat to under section.

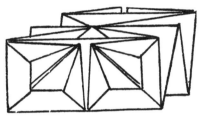

FIG. 203

To open the box, study Fig. 53.

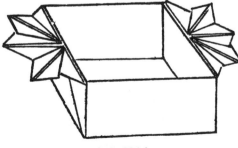

FIG. 204 A

Finished box.

FIG. 204 B

Finished box when folded flat.

TABLE

This is a strong and attractive table that a little girl can make to order in any size to furnish her doll's house. It looks very real and pretty in wood-grained paper as well as in other colors.

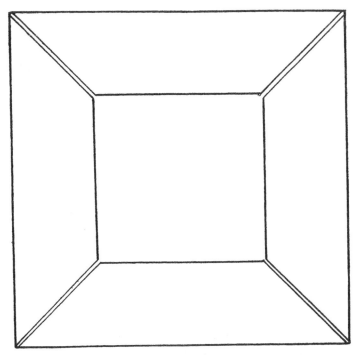

FIG. 205

Follow directions for Figs. 89, 90 and 91 to get illustration, Fig. 205.

Turn Fig. 205 over to the other side.

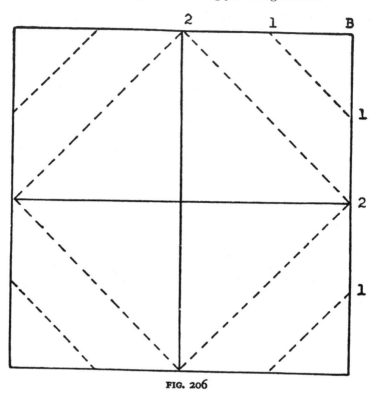

FIG. 206

Fold on dotted line 1-1 by bringing point B on dotted line 2; then roll over and fold again on dotted line 2-2. Crease firmly on the folds.

Repeat the above directions to the other three corners.

When finished it will look as shown in Fig. 207.

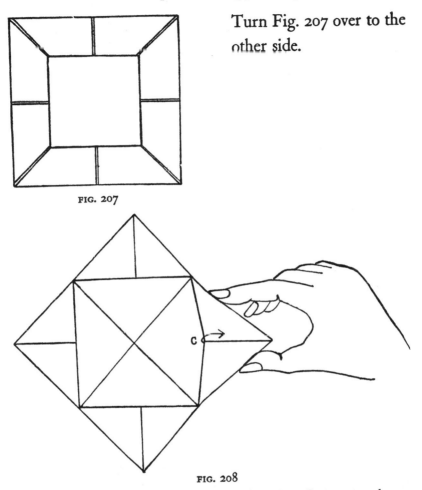

Turn Fig. 207 over to the other side.

FIG. 207

FIG. 208

Place corner between thumb and index finger as shown here (Fig. 208). Push point C upward (with left finger) and at the same time close your right thumb and index finger together. (When finished the corner will look as in Fig. 209.)

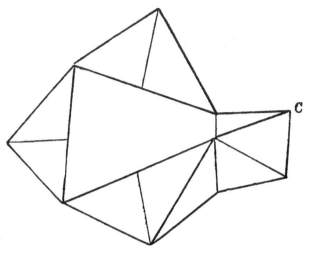

FIG. 209

Repeat directions for Fig. 208 to the other three corners.

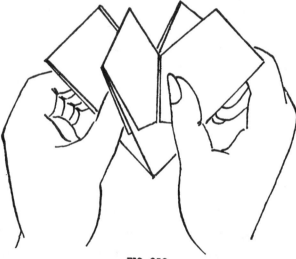

FIG. 210

Hold model in hands as shown here (Fig. 210) and carefully push the sides together until closed up flat. (See Fig. 211.)

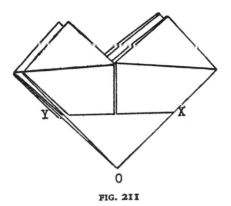

Push up line X-Y and unfold the little hidden triangle, bringing its point down to point O.

FIG. 211

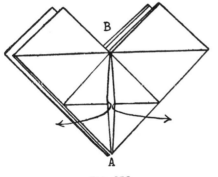

Open out edges apart as indicated by arrows, to the left and right.

Bring point A to point B.

See illustration in Fig. 213.

FIG. 212

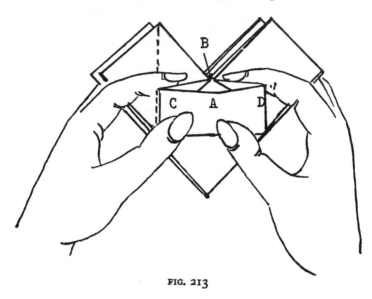

FIG. 213

Fold and crease firmly on the dotted line. Unfold. Take out corner C. Fold again.

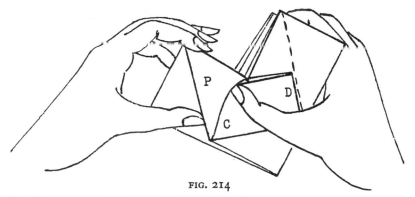

FIG. 214

Tuck corner C into the pocket P.

Fold and crease firmly on the dotted line. Unfold.

Take out corner D. Fold again.

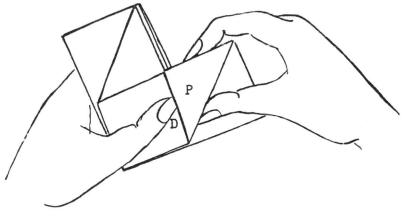

FIG. 215

Tuck corner D into pocket P.

When finished turn Fig. 215 over to the other side and repeat directions for Figs. 211, 212, 213, 214 and 215.

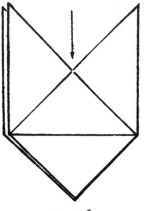

FIG. 216

Open table where indicated by arrow. (Do it carefully so as not to break the foldings.)

Ease the table top into a square shape and crease into position.

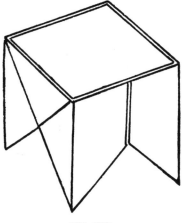

FIG. 217

Finished table.

THREE PIECE LIVING ROOM SET

It is most attractive to make these sofas with patterned or colored papers.

A square is used to make a single sofa, and a rectangle of any length, with the same width (A-B) as the square, is used for a large sofa.

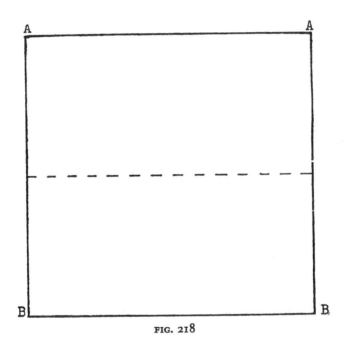

FIG. 218

Fold the paper on the dotted line, bringing line B-B to line A-A.

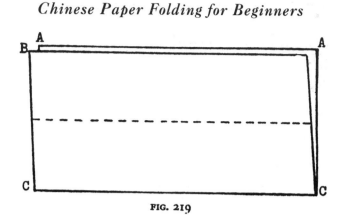

FIG. 219

Crease and fold on dotted line, bringing line B-B to line C-C. Turn over, placing C-C at top.

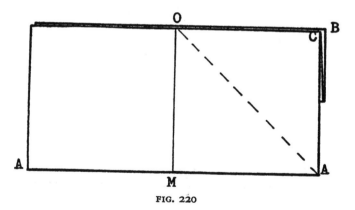

FIG. 220

Fold on the dotted line by bringing line O-C to line O-M.

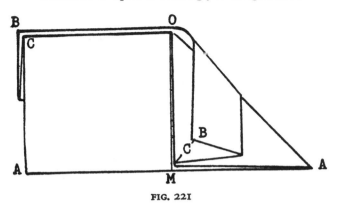

FIG. 221

Bring point B to point O and crease on the dotted line. (See Fig. 222.)

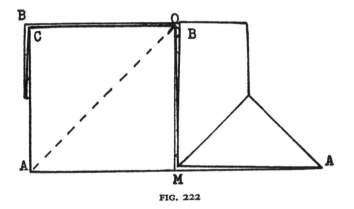

FIG. 222

Repeat directions for Fig. 220 and Fig. 221 to the left side.

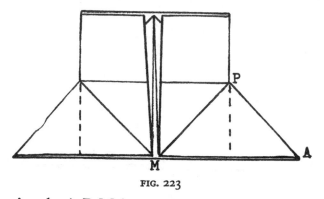

FIG. 223

Open triangle A P M into a square.

Repeat same on left side. (See position of point A in Fig. 224.)

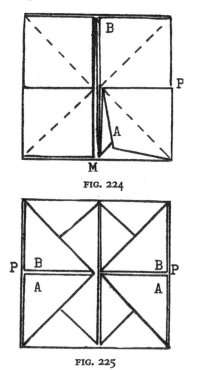

FIG. 224

Fold on the dotted lines by bringing points B and A to point P.

Repeat same on left side.

FIG. 225

Turn Fig. 225 over to the other side.

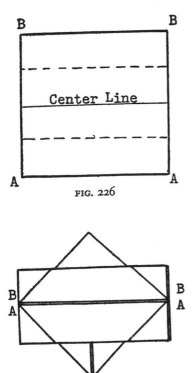

FIG. 226

Fold on the dotted lines by bringing line B-B and line A-A to center line.

FIG. 227

Turn Fig. 227 over to the other side.

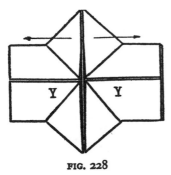

FIG. 228

Hold flaps Y firmly. Then open the sofa as indicated by the arrows.

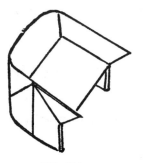

Finished single sofa.

FIG. 229

FIG. 230

The set.

A CATALOG OF SELECTED

DOVER BOOKS

IN ALL FIELDS OF INTEREST

A CATALOG OF SELECTED DOVER
BOOKS IN ALL FIELDS OF INTEREST

CONCERNING THE SPIRITUAL IN ART, Wassily Kandinsky. Pioneering work by father of abstract art. Thoughts on color theory, nature of art. Analysis of earlier masters. 12 illustrations. 80pp. of text. 5⅜ x 8½. 23411-8

ANIMALS: 1,419 Copyright-Free Illustrations of Mammals, Birds, Fish, Insects, etc., Jim Harter (ed.). Clear wood engravings present, in extremely lifelike poses, over 1,000 species of animals. One of the most extensive pictorial sourcebooks of its kind. Captions. Index. 284pp. 9 x 12. 23766-4

CELTIC ART: The Methods of Construction, George Bain. Simple geometric techniques for making Celtic interlacements, spirals, Kells-type initials, animals, humans, etc. Over 500 illustrations. 160pp. 9 x 12. (Available in U.S. only.) 22923-8

AN ATLAS OF ANATOMY FOR ARTISTS, Fritz Schider. Most thorough reference work on art anatomy in the world. Hundreds of illustrations, including selections from works by Vesalius, Leonardo, Goya, Ingres, Michelangelo, others. 593 illustrations. 192pp. 7⅛ x 10¼. 20241-0

CELTIC HAND STROKE-BY-STROKE (Irish Half-Uncial from "The Book of Kells"): An Arthur Baker Calligraphy Manual, Arthur Baker. Complete guide to creating each letter of the alphabet in distinctive Celtic manner. Covers hand position, strokes, pens, inks, paper, more. Illustrated. 48pp. 8¼ x 11. 24336-2

EASY ORIGAMI, John Montroll. Charming collection of 32 projects (hat, cup, pelican, piano, swan, many more) specially designed for the novice origami hobbyist. Clearly illustrated easy-to-follow instructions insure that even beginning papercrafters will achieve successful results. 48pp. 8¼ x 11. 27298-2

THE COMPLETE BOOK OF BIRDHOUSE CONSTRUCTION FOR WOOD-WORKERS, Scott D. Campbell. Detailed instructions, illustrations, tables. Also data on bird habitat and instinct patterns. Bibliography. 3 tables. 63 illustrations in 15 figures. 48pp. 5¼ x 8½. 24407-5

BLOOMINGDALE'S ILLUSTRATED 1886 CATALOG: Fashions, Dry Goods and Housewares, Bloomingdale Brothers. Famed merchants' extremely rare catalog depicting about 1,700 products: clothing, housewares, firearms, dry goods, jewelry, more. Invaluable for dating, identifying vintage items. Also, copyright-free graphics for artists, designers. Co-published with Henry Ford Museum & Greenfield Village. 160pp. 8¼ x 11. 25780-0

HISTORIC COSTUME IN PICTURES, Braun & Schneider. Over 1,450 costumed figures in clearly detailed engravings—from dawn of civilization to end of 19th century. Captions. Many folk costumes. 256pp. 8⅜ x 11¾. 23150-X

STICKLEY CRAFTSMAN FURNITURE CATALOGS, Gustav Stickley and L. & J. G. Stickley. Beautiful, functional furniture in two authentic catalogs from 1910. 594 illustrations, including 277 photos, show settles, rockers, armchairs, reclining chairs, bookcases, desks, tables. 183pp. 6½ x 9¼. 23838-5

AMERICAN LOCOMOTIVES IN HISTORIC PHOTOGRAPHS: 1858 to 1949, Ron Ziel (ed.). A rare collection of 126 meticulously detailed official photographs, called "builder portraits," of American locomotives that majestically chronicle the rise of steam locomotive power in America. Introduction. Detailed captions. xi+ 129pp. 9 x 12. 27393-8

AMERICA'S LIGHTHOUSES: An Illustrated History, Francis Ross Holland, Jr. Delightfully written, profusely illustrated fact-filled survey of over 200 American lighthouses since 1716. History, anecdotes, technological advances, more. 240pp. 8 x 10¾. 25576-X

TOWARDS A NEW ARCHITECTURE, Le Corbusier. Pioneering manifesto by founder of "International School." Technical and aesthetic theories, views of industry, economics, relation of form to function, "mass-production split" and much more. Profusely illustrated. 320pp. 6⅛ x 9¼. (Available in U.S. only.) 25023-7

HOW THE OTHER HALF LIVES, Jacob Riis. Famous journalistic record, exposing poverty and degradation of New York slums around 1900, by major social reformer. 100 striking and influential photographs. 233pp. 10 x 7⅞. 22012-5

FRUIT KEY AND TWIG KEY TO TREES AND SHRUBS, William M. Harlow. One of the handiest and most widely used identification aids. Fruit key covers 120 deciduous and evergreen species; twig key 160 deciduous species. Easily used. Over 300 photographs. 126pp. 5⅜ x 8½. 20511-8

COMMON BIRD SONGS, Dr. Donald J. Borror. Songs of 60 most common U.S. birds: robins, sparrows, cardinals, bluejays, finches, more—arranged in order of increasing complexity. Up to 9 variations of songs of each species.
Cassette and manual 99911-4

ORCHIDS AS HOUSE PLANTS, Rebecca Tyson Northen. Grow cattleyas and many other kinds of orchids—in a window, in a case, or under artificial light. 63 illustrations. 148pp. 5⅜ x 8½. 23261-1

MONSTER MAZES, Dave Phillips. Masterful mazes at four levels of difficulty. Avoid deadly perils and evil creatures to find magical treasures. Solutions for all 32 exciting illustrated puzzles. 48pp. 8¼ x 11. 26005-4

MOZART'S DON GIOVANNI (DOVER OPERA LIBRETTO SERIES), Wolfgang Amadeus Mozart. Introduced and translated by Ellen H. Bleiler. Standard Italian libretto, with complete English translation. Convenient and thoroughly portable—an ideal companion for reading along with a recording or the performance itself. Introduction. List of characters. Plot summary. 121pp. 5¼ x 8½. 24944-1

TECHNICAL MANUAL AND DICTIONARY OF CLASSICAL BALLET, Gail Grant. Defines, explains, comments on steps, movements, poses and concepts. 15-page pictorial section. Basic book for student, viewer. 127pp. 5⅜ x 8½. 21843-0

THE CLARINET AND CLARINET PLAYING, David Pino. Lively, comprehensive work features suggestions about technique, musicianship, and musical interpretation, as well as guidelines for teaching, making your own reeds, and preparing for public performance. Includes an intriguing look at clarinet history. "A godsend," *The Clarinet,* Journal of the International Clarinet Society. Appendixes. 7 illus. 320pp. 5⅜ x 8½. 40270-3

HOLLYWOOD GLAMOR PORTRAITS, John Kobal (ed.). 145 photos from 1926-49. Harlow, Gable, Bogart, Bacall; 94 stars in all. Full background on photographers, technical aspects. 160pp. 8⅜ x 11¼. 23352-9

THE ANNOTATED CASEY AT THE BAT: A Collection of Ballads about the Mighty Casey/Third, Revised Edition, Martin Gardner (ed.). Amusing sequels and parodies of one of America's best-loved poems: Casey's Revenge, Why Casey Whiffed, Casey's Sister at the Bat, others. 256pp. 5⅜ x 8½. 28598-7

THE RAVEN AND OTHER FAVORITE POEMS, Edgar Allan Poe. Over 40 of the author's most memorable poems: "The Bells," "Ulalume," "Israfel," "To Helen," "The Conqueror Worm," "Eldorado," "Annabel Lee," many more. Alphabetic lists of titles and first lines. 64pp. 5$^{3}/_{16}$ x 8¼. 26685-0

PERSONAL MEMOIRS OF U. S. GRANT, Ulysses Simpson Grant. Intelligent, deeply moving firsthand account of Civil War campaigns, considered by many the finest military memoirs ever written. Includes letters, historic photographs, maps and more. 528pp. 6⅛ x 9¼. 28587-1

ANCIENT EGYPTIAN MATERIALS AND INDUSTRIES, A. Lucas and J. Harris. Fascinating, comprehensive, thoroughly documented text describes this ancient civilization's vast resources and the processes that incorporated them in daily life, including the use of animal products, building materials, cosmetics, perfumes and incense, fibers, glazed ware, glass and its manufacture, materials used in the mummification process, and much more. 544pp. 6⅛ x 9¼. (Available in U.S. only.) 40446-3

RUSSIAN STORIES/RUSSKIE RASSKAZY: A Dual-Language Book, edited by Gleb Struve. Twelve tales by such masters as Chekhov, Tolstoy, Dostoevsky, Pushkin, others. Excellent word-for-word English translations on facing pages, plus teaching and study aids, Russian/English vocabulary, biographical/critical introductions, more. 416pp. 5⅜ x 8½. 26244-8

PHILADELPHIA THEN AND NOW: 60 Sites Photographed in the Past and Present, Kenneth Finkel and Susan Oyama. Rare photographs of City Hall, Logan Square, Independence Hall, Betsy Ross House, other landmarks juxtaposed with contemporary views. Captures changing face of historic city. Introduction. Captions. 128pp. 8¼ x 11. 25790-8

AIA ARCHITECTURAL GUIDE TO NASSAU AND SUFFOLK COUNTIES, LONG ISLAND, The American Institute of Architects, Long Island Chapter, and the Society for the Preservation of Long Island Antiquities. Comprehensive, well-researched and generously illustrated volume brings to life over three centuries of Long Island's great architectural heritage. More than 240 photographs with authoritative, extensively detailed captions. 176pp. 8¼ x 11. 26946-9

NORTH AMERICAN INDIAN LIFE: Customs and Traditions of 23 Tribes, Elsie Clews Parsons (ed.). 27 fictionalized essays by noted anthropologists examine religion, customs, government, additional facets of life among the Winnebago, Crow, Zuni, Eskimo, other tribes. 480pp. 6⅛ x 9¼. 27377-6

FRANK LLOYD WRIGHT'S DANA HOUSE, Donald Hoffmann. Pictorial essay of residential masterpiece with over 160 interior and exterior photos, plans, elevations, sketches and studies. 128pp. $9^1/_4$ x $10^3/_4$. 29120-0

THE MALE AND FEMALE FIGURE IN MOTION: 60 Classic Photographic Sequences, Eadweard Muybridge. 60 true-action photographs of men and women walking, running, climbing, bending, turning, etc., reproduced from rare 19th-century masterpiece. vi + 121pp. 9 x 12. 24745-7

1001 QUESTIONS ANSWERED ABOUT THE SEASHORE, N. J. Berrill and Jacquelyn Berrill. Queries answered about dolphins, sea snails, sponges, starfish, fishes, shore birds, many others. Covers appearance, breeding, growth, feeding, much more. 305pp. $5^1/_4$ x $8^1/_4$. 23366-9

ATTRACTING BIRDS TO YOUR YARD, William J. Weber. Easy-to-follow guide offers advice on how to attract the greatest diversity of birds: birdhouses, feeders, water and waterers, much more. 96pp. $5^3/_{16}$ x $8^1/_4$. 28927-3

MEDICINAL AND OTHER USES OF NORTH AMERICAN PLANTS: A Historical Survey with Special Reference to the Eastern Indian Tribes, Charlotte Erichsen-Brown. Chronological historical citations document 500 years of usage of plants, trees, shrubs native to eastern Canada, northeastern U.S. Also complete identifying information. 343 illustrations. 544pp. $6^1/_2$ x $9^1/_4$. 25951-X

STORYBOOK MAZES, Dave Phillips. 23 stories and mazes on two-page spreads: Wizard of Oz, Treasure Island, Robin Hood, etc. Solutions. 64pp. $8^1/_4$ x 11. 23628-5

AMERICAN NEGRO SONGS: 230 Folk Songs and Spirituals, Religious and Secular, John W. Work. This authoritative study traces the African influences of songs sung and played by black Americans at work, in church, and as entertainment. The author discusses the lyric significance of such songs as "Swing Low, Sweet Chariot," "John Henry," and others and offers the words and music for 230 songs. Bibliography. Index of Song Titles. 272pp. $6^1/_2$ x $9^1/_4$. 40271-1

MOVIE-STAR PORTRAITS OF THE FORTIES, John Kobal (ed.). 163 glamor, studio photos of 106 stars of the 1940s: Rita Hayworth, Ava Gardner, Marlon Brando, Clark Gable, many more. 176pp. $8^3/_8$ x $11^1/_4$. 23546-7

BENCHLEY LOST AND FOUND, Robert Benchley. Finest humor from early 30s, about pet peeves, child psychologists, post office and others. Mostly unavailable elsewhere. 73 illustrations by Peter Arno and others. 183pp. $5^3/_8$ x $8^1/_2$. 22410-4

YEKL and THE IMPORTED BRIDEGROOM AND OTHER STORIES OF YIDDISH NEW YORK, Abraham Cahan. Film Hester Street based on *Yekl* (1896). Novel, other stories among first about Jewish immigrants on N.Y.'s East Side. 240pp. $5^3/_8$ x $8^1/_2$. 22427-9

SELECTED POEMS, Walt Whitman. Generous sampling from *Leaves of Grass*. Twenty-four poems include "I Hear America Singing," "Song of the Open Road," "I Sing the Body Electric," "When Lilacs Last in the Dooryard Bloom'd," "O Captain! My Captain!"–all reprinted from an authoritative edition. Lists of titles and first lines. 128pp. $5^3/_{16}$ x $8^1/_4$. 26878-0

THE BEST TALES OF HOFFMANN, E. T. A. Hoffmann. 10 of Hoffmann's most important stories: "Nutcracker and the King of Mice," "The Golden Flowerpot," etc. 458pp. 5⅜ x 8½. 21793-0

FROM FETISH TO GOD IN ANCIENT EGYPT, E. A. Wallis Budge. Rich detailed survey of Egyptian conception of "God" and gods, magic, cult of animals, Osiris, more. Also, superb English translations of hymns and legends. 240 illustrations. 545pp. 5⅜ x 8½. 25803-3

FRENCH STORIES/CONTES FRANÇAIS: A Dual-Language Book, Wallace Fowlie. Ten stories by French masters, Voltaire to Camus: "Micromegas" by Voltaire; "The Atheist's Mass" by Balzac; "Minuet" by de Maupassant; "The Guest" by Camus, six more. Excellent English translations on facing pages. Also French-English vocabulary list, exercises, more. 352pp. 5⅜ x 8½. 26443-2

CHICAGO AT THE TURN OF THE CENTURY IN PHOTOGRAPHS: 122 Historic Views from the Collections of the Chicago Historical Society, Larry A. Viskochil. Rare large-format prints offer detailed views of City Hall, State Street, the Loop, Hull House, Union Station, many other landmarks, circa 1904-1913. Introduction. Captions. Maps. 144pp. 9⅜ x 12¼. 24656-6

OLD BROOKLYN IN EARLY PHOTOGRAPHS, 1865-1929, William Lee Younger. Luna Park, Gravesend race track, construction of Grand Army Plaza, moving of Hotel Brighton, etc. 157 previously unpublished photographs. 165pp. 8⅞ x 11¾. 23587-4

THE MYTHS OF THE NORTH AMERICAN INDIANS, Lewis Spence. Rich anthology of the myths and legends of the Algonquins, Iroquois, Pawnees and Sioux, prefaced by an extensive historical and ethnological commentary. 36 illustrations. 480pp. 5⅜ x 8½. 25967-6

AN ENCYCLOPEDIA OF BATTLES: Accounts of Over 1,560 Battles from 1479 B.C. to the Present, David Eggenberger. Essential details of every major battle in recorded history from the first battle of Megiddo in 1479 B.C. to Grenada in 1984. List of Battle Maps. New Appendix covering the years 1967-1984. Index. 99 illustrations. 544pp. 6½ x 9¼. 24913-1

SAILING ALONE AROUND THE WORLD, Captain Joshua Slocum. First man to sail around the world, alone, in small boat. One of great feats of seamanship told in delightful manner. 67 illustrations. 294pp. 5⅜ x 8½. 20326-3

ANARCHISM AND OTHER ESSAYS, Emma Goldman. Powerful, penetrating, prophetic essays on direct action, role of minorities, prison reform, puritan hypocrisy, violence, etc. 271pp. 5⅜ x 8½. 22484-8

MYTHS OF THE HINDUS AND BUDDHISTS, Ananda K. Coomaraswamy and Sister Nivedita. Great stories of the epics; deeds of Krishna, Shiva, taken from puranas, Vedas, folk tales; etc. 32 illustrations. 400pp. 5⅜ x 8½. 21759-0

THE TRAUMA OF BIRTH, Otto Rank. Rank's controversial thesis that anxiety neurosis is caused by profound psychological trauma which occurs at birth. 256pp. 5⅜ x 8½. 27974-X

A THEOLOGICO-POLITICAL TREATISE, Benedict Spinoza. Also contains unfinished Political Treatise. Great classic on religious liberty, theory of government on common consent. R. Elwes translation. Total of 421pp. 5⅜ x 8½. 20249-6

MY BONDAGE AND MY FREEDOM, Frederick Douglass. Born a slave, Douglass became outspoken force in antislavery movement. The best of Douglass' autobiographies. Graphic description of slave life. 464pp. 5⅜ x 8½. 22457-0

FOLLOWING THE EQUATOR: A Journey Around the World, Mark Twain. Fascinating humorous account of 1897 voyage to Hawaii, Australia, India, New Zealand, etc. Ironic, bemused reports on peoples, customs, climate, flora and fauna, politics, much more. 197 illustrations. 720pp. 5⅜ x 8½. 26113-1

THE PEOPLE CALLED SHAKERS, Edward D. Andrews. Definitive study of Shakers: origins, beliefs, practices, dances, social organization, furniture and crafts, etc. 33 illustrations. 351pp. 5⅜ x 8½. 21081-2

THE MYTHS OF GREECE AND ROME, H. A. Guerber. A classic of mythology, generously illustrated, long prized for its simple, graphic, accurate retelling of the principal myths of Greece and Rome, and for its commentary on their origins and significance. With 64 illustrations by Michelangelo, Raphael, Titian, Rubens, Canova, Bernini and others. 480pp. 5⅜ x 8½. 27584-1

PSYCHOLOGY OF MUSIC, Carl E. Seashore. Classic work discusses music as a medium from psychological viewpoint. Clear treatment of physical acoustics, auditory apparatus, sound perception, development of musical skills, nature of musical feeling, host of other topics. 88 figures. 408pp. 5⅜ x 8½. 21851-1

THE PHILOSOPHY OF HISTORY, Georg W. Hegel. Great classic of Western thought develops concept that history is not chance but rational process, the evolution of freedom. 457pp. 5⅜ x 8½. 20112-0

THE BOOK OF TEA, Kakuzo Okakura. Minor classic of the Orient: entertaining, charming explanation, interpretation of traditional Japanese culture in terms of tea ceremony. 94pp. 5⅜ x 8½. 20070-1

LIFE IN ANCIENT EGYPT, Adolf Erman. Fullest, most thorough, detailed older account with much not in more recent books, domestic life, religion, magic, medicine, commerce, much more. Many illustrations reproduce tomb paintings, carvings, hieroglyphs, etc. 597pp. 5⅜ x 8½. 22632-8

SUNDIALS, Their Theory and Construction, Albert Waugh. Far and away the best, most thorough coverage of ideas, mathematics concerned, types, construction, adjusting anywhere. Simple, nontechnical treatment allows even children to build several of these dials. Over 100 illustrations. 230pp. 5⅜ x 8½. 22947-5

THEORETICAL HYDRODYNAMICS, L. M. Milne-Thomson. Classic exposition of the mathematical theory of fluid motion, applicable to both hydrodynamics and aerodynamics. Over 600 exercises. 768pp. 6⅛ x 9¼. 68970-0

SONGS OF EXPERIENCE: Facsimile Reproduction with 26 Plates in Full Color, William Blake. 26 full-color plates from a rare 1826 edition. Includes "The Tyger," "London," "Holy Thursday," and other poems. Printed text of poems. 48pp. 5¼ x 7. 24636-1

OLD-TIME VIGNETTES IN FULL COLOR, Carol Belanger Grafton (ed.). Over 390 charming, often sentimental illustrations, selected from archives of Victorian graphics—pretty women posing, children playing, food, flowers, kittens and puppies, smiling cherubs, birds and butterflies, much more. All copyright-free. 48pp. 9¼ x 12¼. 27269-9

PERSPECTIVE FOR ARTISTS, Rex Vicat Cole. Depth, perspective of sky and sea, shadows, much more, not usually covered. 391 diagrams, 81 reproductions of drawings and paintings. 279pp. 5⅜ x 8½. 22487-2

DRAWING THE LIVING FIGURE, Joseph Sheppard. Innovative approach to artistic anatomy focuses on specifics of surface anatomy, rather than muscles and bones. Over 170 drawings of live models in front, back and side views, and in widely varying poses. Accompanying diagrams. 177 illustrations. Introduction. Index. 144pp. 8⅜ x11¼. 26723-7

GOTHIC AND OLD ENGLISH ALPHABETS: 100 Complete Fonts, Dan X. Solo. Add power, elegance to posters, signs, other graphics with 100 stunning copyright-free alphabets: Blackstone, Dolbey, Germania, 97 more–including many lower-case, numerals, punctuation marks. 104pp. 8⅛ x 11. 24695-7

HOW TO DO BEADWORK, Mary White. Fundamental book on craft from simple projects to five-bead chains and woven works. 106 illustrations. 142pp. 5⅜ x 8. 20697-1

THE BOOK OF WOOD CARVING, Charles Marshall Sayers. Finest book for beginners discusses fundamentals and offers 34 designs. "Absolutely first rate . . . well thought out and well executed."–E. J. Tangerman. 118pp. 7¾ x 10⅝. 23654-4

ILLUSTRATED CATALOG OF CIVIL WAR MILITARY GOODS: Union Army Weapons, Insignia, Uniform Accessories, and Other Equipment, Schuyler, Hartley, and Graham. Rare, profusely illustrated 1846 catalog includes Union Army uniform and dress regulations, arms and ammunition, coats, insignia, flags, swords, rifles, etc. 226 illustrations. 160pp. 9 x 12. 24939-5

WOMEN'S FASHIONS OF THE EARLY 1900s: An Unabridged Republication of "New York Fashions, 1909," National Cloak & Suit Co. Rare catalog of mail-order fashions documents women's and children's clothing styles shortly after the turn of the century. Captions offer full descriptions, prices. Invaluable resource for fashion, costume historians. Approximately 725 illustrations. 128pp. 8⅜ x 11¼. 27276-1

THE 1912 AND 1915 GUSTAV STICKLEY FURNITURE CATALOGS, Gustav Stickley. With over 200 detailed illustrations and descriptions, these two catalogs are essential reading and reference materials and identification guides for Stickley furniture. Captions cite materials, dimensions and prices. 112pp. 6½ x 9¼. 26676-1

EARLY AMERICAN LOCOMOTIVES, John H. White, Jr. Finest locomotive engravings from early 19th century: historical (1804–74), main-line (after 1870), special, foreign, etc. 147 plates. 142pp. 11⅜ x 8¼. 22772-3

THE TALL SHIPS OF TODAY IN PHOTOGRAPHS, Frank O. Braynard. Lavishly illustrated tribute to nearly 100 majestic contemporary sailing vessels: Amerigo Vespucci, Clearwater, Constitution, Eagle, Mayflower, Sea Cloud, Victory, many more. Authoritative captions provide statistics, background on each ship. 190 black-and-white photographs and illustrations. Introduction. 128pp. 8⅞ x 11¾. 27163-3

LITTLE BOOK OF EARLY AMERICAN CRAFTS AND TRADES, Peter Stockham (ed.). 1807 children's book explains crafts and trades: baker, hatter, cooper, potter, and many others. 23 copperplate illustrations. 140pp. 4⅝ x 6. 23336-7

VICTORIAN FASHIONS AND COSTUMES FROM HARPER'S BAZAR, 1867–1898, Stella Blum (ed.). Day costumes, evening wear, sports clothes, shoes, hats, other accessories in over 1,000 detailed engravings. 320pp. 9⅜ x 12¼. 22990-4

GUSTAV STICKLEY, THE CRAFTSMAN, Mary Ann Smith. Superb study surveys broad scope of Stickley's achievement, especially in architecture. Design philosophy, rise and fall of the Craftsman empire, descriptions and floor plans for many Craftsman houses, more. 86 black-and-white halftones. 31 line illustrations. Introduction 208pp. 6½ x 9¼. 27210-9

THE LONG ISLAND RAIL ROAD IN EARLY PHOTOGRAPHS, Ron Ziel. Over 220 rare photos, informative text document origin (1844) and development of rail service on Long Island. Vintage views of early trains, locomotives, stations, passengers, crews, much more. Captions. 8⅞ x 11¾. 26301-0

VOYAGE OF THE LIBERDADE, Joshua Slocum. Great 19th-century mariner's thrilling, first-hand account of the wreck of his ship off South America, the 35-foot boat he built from the wreckage, and its remarkable voyage home. 128pp. 5⅜ x 8½. 40022-0

TEN BOOKS ON ARCHITECTURE, Vitruvius. The most important book ever written on architecture. Early Roman aesthetics, technology, classical orders, site selection, all other aspects. Morgan translation. 331pp. 5⅜ x 8½. 20645-9

THE HUMAN FIGURE IN MOTION, Eadweard Muybridge. More than 4,500 stopped-action photos, in action series, showing undraped men, women, children jumping, lying down, throwing, sitting, wrestling, carrying, etc. 390pp. 7⅞ x 10⅝. 20204-6 Clothbd.

TREES OF THE EASTERN AND CENTRAL UNITED STATES AND CANADA, William M. Harlow. Best one-volume guide to 140 trees. Full descriptions, woodlore, range, etc. Over 600 illustrations. Handy size. 288pp. 4½ x 6⅜. 20395-6

SONGS OF WESTERN BIRDS, Dr. Donald J. Borror. Complete song and call repertoire of 60 western species, including flycatchers, juncoes, cactus wrens, many more—includes fully illustrated booklet. Cassette and manual 99913-0

GROWING AND USING HERBS AND SPICES, Milo Miloradovich. Versatile handbook provides all the information needed for cultivation and use of all the herbs and spices available in North America. 4 illustrations. Index. Glossary. 236pp. 5⅜ x 8½. 25058-X

BIG BOOK OF MAZES AND LABYRINTHS, Walter Shepherd. 50 mazes and labyrinths in all—classical, solid, ripple, and more—in one great volume. Perfect inexpensive puzzler for clever youngsters. Full solutions. 112pp. 8⅛ x 11. 22951-3

CATALOG OF DOVER BOOKS

PIANO TUNING, J. Cree Fischer. Clearest, best book for beginner, amateur. Simple repairs, raising dropped notes, tuning by easy method of flattened fifths. No previous skills needed. 4 illustrations. 201pp. 5⅜ x 8½. 23267-0

HINTS TO SINGERS, Lillian Nordica. Selecting the right teacher, developing confidence, overcoming stage fright, and many other important skills receive thoughtful discussion in this indispensible guide, written by a world-famous diva of four decades' experience. 96pp. 5⅜ x 8½. 40094-8

THE COMPLETE NONSENSE OF EDWARD LEAR, Edward Lear. All nonsense limericks, zany alphabets, Owl and Pussycat, songs, nonsense botany, etc., illustrated by Lear. Total of 320pp. 5⅜ x 8½. (Available in U.S. only.) 20167-8

VICTORIAN PARLOUR POETRY: An Annotated Anthology, Michael R. Turner. 117 gems by Longfellow, Tennyson, Browning, many lesser-known poets. "The Village Blacksmith," "Curfew Must Not Ring Tonight," "Only a Baby Small," dozens more, often difficult to find elsewhere. Index of poets, titles, first lines. xxiii + 325pp. 5⅝ x 8¼. 27044-0

DUBLINERS, James Joyce. Fifteen stories offer vivid, tightly focused observations of the lives of Dublin's poorer classes. At least one, "The Dead," is considered a masterpiece. Reprinted complete and unabridged from standard edition. 160pp. 5 3/16 x 8¼. 26870-5

GREAT WEIRD TALES: 14 Stories by Lovecraft, Blackwood, Machen and Others, S. T. Joshi (ed.). 14 spellbinding tales, including "The Sin Eater," by Fiona McLeod, "The Eye Above the Mantel," by Frank Belknap Long, as well as renowned works by R. H. Barlow, Lord Dunsany, Arthur Machen, W. C. Morrow and eight other masters of the genre. 256pp. 5⅜ x 8½. (Available in U.S. only.) 40436-6

THE BOOK OF THE SACRED MAGIC OF ABRAMELIN THE MAGE, translated by S. MacGregor Mathers. Medieval manuscript of ceremonial magic. Basic document in Aleister Crowley, Golden Dawn groups. 268pp. 5⅜ x 8½. 23211-5

NEW RUSSIAN-ENGLISH AND ENGLISH-RUSSIAN DICTIONARY, M. A. O'Brien. This is a remarkably handy Russian dictionary, containing a surprising amount of information, including over 70,000 entries. 366pp. 4½ x 6⅛. 20208-9

HISTORIC HOMES OF THE AMERICAN PRESIDENTS, Second, Revised Edition, Irvin Haas. A traveler's guide to American Presidential homes, most open to the public, depicting and describing homes occupied by every American President from George Washington to George Bush. With visiting hours, admission charges, travel routes. 175 photographs. Index. 160pp. 8¼ x 11. 26751-2

NEW YORK IN THE FORTIES, Andreas Feininger. 162 brilliant photographs by the well-known photographer, formerly with *Life* magazine. Commuters, shoppers, Times Square at night, much else from city at its peak. Captions by John von Hartz. 181pp. 9¼ x 10¾. 23585-8

INDIAN SIGN LANGUAGE, William Tomkins. Over 525 signs developed by Sioux and other tribes. Written instructions and diagrams. Also 290 pictographs. 111pp. 6⅛ x 9¼. 22029-X

CATALOG OF DOVER BOOKS

ANATOMY: A Complete Guide for Artists, Joseph Sheppard. A master of figure drawing shows artists how to render human anatomy convincingly. Over 460 illustrations. 224pp. 8⅜ x 11¼. 27279-6

MEDIEVAL CALLIGRAPHY: Its History and Technique, Marc Drogin. Spirited history, comprehensive instruction manual covers 13 styles (ca. 4th century through 15th). Excellent photographs; directions for duplicating medieval techniques with modern tools. 224pp. 8⅜ x 11¼. 26142-5

DRIED FLOWERS: How to Prepare Them, Sarah Whitlock and Martha Rankin. Complete instructions on how to use silica gel, meal and borax, perlite aggregate, sand and borax, glycerine and water to create attractive permanent flower arrangements. 12 illustrations. 32pp. 5⅜ x 8½. 21802-3

EASY-TO-MAKE BIRD FEEDERS FOR WOODWORKERS, Scott D. Campbell. Detailed, simple-to-use guide for designing, constructing, caring for and using feeders. Text, illustrations for 12 classic and contemporary designs. 96pp. 5⅜ x 8½. 25847-5

SCOTTISH WONDER TALES FROM MYTH AND LEGEND, Donald A. Mackenzie. 16 lively tales tell of giants rumbling down mountainsides, of a magic wand that turns stone pillars into warriors, of gods and goddesses, evil hags, powerful forces and more. 240pp. 5⅜ x 8½. 29677-6

THE HISTORY OF UNDERCLOTHES, C. Willett Cunnington and Phyllis Cunnington. Fascinating, well-documented survey covering six centuries of English undergarments, enhanced with over 100 illustrations: 12th-century laced-up bodice, footed long drawers (1795), 19th-century bustles, 19th-century corsets for men, Victorian "bust improvers," much more. 272pp. 5⅝ x 8¼. 27124-2

ARTS AND CRAFTS FURNITURE: The Complete Brooks Catalog of 1912, Brooks Manufacturing Co. Photos and detailed descriptions of more than 150 now very collectible furniture designs from the Arts and Crafts movement depict davenports, settees, buffets, desks, tables, chairs, bedsteads, dressers and more, all built of solid, quarter-sawed oak. Invaluable for students and enthusiasts of antiques, Americana and the decorative arts. 80pp. 6½ x 9¼. 27471-3

WILBUR AND ORVILLE: A Biography of the Wright Brothers, Fred Howard. Definitive, crisply written study tells the full story of the brothers' lives and work. A vividly written biography, unparalleled in scope and color, that also captures the spirit of an extraordinary era. 560pp. 6⅛ x 9¼. 40297-5

THE ARTS OF THE SAILOR: Knotting, Splicing and Ropework, Hervey Garrett Smith. Indispensable shipboard reference covers tools, basic knots and useful hitches; handsewing and canvas work, more. Over 100 illustrations. Delightful reading for sea lovers. 256pp. 5⅜ x 8½. 26440-8

FRANK LLOYD WRIGHT'S FALLINGWATER: The House and Its History, Second, Revised Edition, Donald Hoffmann. A total revision–both in text and illustrations–of the standard document on Fallingwater, the boldest, most personal architectural statement of Wright's mature years, updated with valuable new material from the recently opened Frank Lloyd Wright Archives. "Fascinating"–*The New York Times*. 116 illustrations. 128pp. 9¼ x 10¾. 27430-6

CATALOG OF DOVER BOOKS

PHOTOGRAPHIC SKETCHBOOK OF THE CIVIL WAR, Alexander Gardner. 100 photos taken on field during the Civil War. Famous shots of Manassas Harper's Ferry, Lincoln, Richmond, slave pens, etc. 244pp. 10⅝ x 8¼. 22731-6

FIVE ACRES AND INDEPENDENCE, Maurice G. Kains. Great back-to-the-land classic explains basics of self-sufficient farming. The one book to get. 95 illustrations. 397pp. 5⅜ x 8½. 20974-1

SONGS OF EASTERN BIRDS, Dr. Donald J. Borror. Songs and calls of 60 species most common to eastern U.S.: warblers, woodpeckers, flycatchers, thrushes, larks, many more in high-quality recording. Cassette and manual 99912-2

A MODERN HERBAL, Margaret Grieve. Much the fullest, most exact, most useful compilation of herbal material. Gigantic alphabetical encyclopedia, from aconite to zedoary, gives botanical information, medical properties, folklore, economic uses, much else. Indispensable to serious reader. 161 illustrations. 888pp. 6½ x 9¼. 2-vol. set. (Available in U.S. only.) Vol. I: 22798-7
Vol. II: 22799-5

HIDDEN TREASURE MAZE BOOK, Dave Phillips. Solve 34 challenging mazes accompanied by heroic tales of adventure. Evil dragons, people-eating plants, blood-thirsty giants, many more dangerous adversaries lurk at every twist and turn. 34 mazes, stories, solutions. 48pp. 8¼ x 11. 24566-7

LETTERS OF W. A. MOZART, Wolfgang A. Mozart. Remarkable letters show bawdy wit, humor, imagination, musical insights, contemporary musical world; includes some letters from Leopold Mozart. 276pp. 5⅜ x 8½. 22859-2

BASIC PRINCIPLES OF CLASSICAL BALLET, Agrippina Vaganova. Great Russian theoretician, teacher explains methods for teaching classical ballet. 118 illustrations. 175pp. 5⅜ x 8½. 22036-2

THE JUMPING FROG, Mark Twain. Revenge edition. The original story of The Celebrated Jumping Frog of Calaveras County, a hapless French translation, and Twain's hilarious "retranslation" from the French. 12 illustrations. 66pp. 5⅜ x 8½. 22686-7

BEST REMEMBERED POEMS, Martin Gardner (ed.). The 126 poems in this superb collection of 19th- and 20th-century British and American verse range from Shelley's "To a Skylark" to the impassioned "Renascence" of Edna St. Vincent Millay and to Edward Lear's whimsical "The Owl and the Pussycat." 224pp. 5⅜ x 8½. 27165-X

COMPLETE SONNETS, William Shakespeare. Over 150 exquisite poems deal with love, friendship, the tyranny of time, beauty's evanescence, death and other themes in language of remarkable power, precision and beauty. Glossary of archaic terms. 80pp. 5³⁄₁₆ x 8¼. 26686-9

THE BATTLES THAT CHANGED HISTORY, Fletcher Pratt. Eminent historian profiles 16 crucial conflicts, ancient to modern, that changed the course of civilization. 352pp. 5⅜ x 8½. 41129-X

THE WIT AND HUMOR OF OSCAR WILDE, Alvin Redman (ed.). More than 1,000 ripostes, paradoxes, wisecracks: Work is the curse of the drinking classes; I can resist everything except temptation; etc. 258pp. 5⅜ x 8½. 20602-5

SHAKESPEARE LEXICON AND QUOTATION DICTIONARY, Alexander Schmidt. Full definitions, locations, shades of meaning in every word in plays and poems. More than 50,000 exact quotations. 1,485pp. 6½ x 9¼. 2-vol. set.
Vol. 1: 22726-X
Vol. 2: 22727-8

SELECTED POEMS, Emily Dickinson. Over 100 best-known, best-loved poems by one of America's foremost poets, reprinted from authoritative early editions. No comparable edition at this price. Index of first lines. 64pp. 5³⁄₁₆ x 8¼. 26466-1

THE INSIDIOUS DR. FU-MANCHU, Sax Rohmer. The first of the popular mystery series introduces a pair of English detectives to their archnemesis, the diabolical Dr. Fu-Manchu. Flavorful atmosphere, fast-paced action, and colorful characters enliven this classic of the genre. 208pp. 5³⁄₁₆ x 8¼. 29898-1

THE MALLEUS MALEFICARUM OF KRAMER AND SPRENGER, translated by Montague Summers. Full text of most important witchhunter's "bible," used by both Catholics and Protestants. 278pp. 6⅝ x 10. 22802-9

SPANISH STORIES/CUENTOS ESPAÑOLES: A Dual-Language Book, Angel Flores (ed.). Unique format offers 13 great stories in Spanish by Cervantes, Borges, others. Faithful English translations on facing pages. 352pp. 5⅜ x 8½. 25399-6

GARDEN CITY, LONG ISLAND, IN EARLY PHOTOGRAPHS, 1869–1919, Mildred H. Smith. Handsome treasury of 118 vintage pictures, accompanied by carefully researched captions, document the Garden City Hotel fire (1899), the Vanderbilt Cup Race (1908), the first airmail flight departing from the Nassau Boulevard Aerodrome (1911), and much more. 96pp. 8⅞ x 11¾. 40669-5

OLD QUEENS, N.Y., IN EARLY PHOTOGRAPHS, Vincent F. Seyfried and William Asadorian. Over 160 rare photographs of Maspeth, Jamaica, Jackson Heights, and other areas. Vintage views of DeWitt Clinton mansion, 1939 World's Fair and more. Captions. 192pp. 8⅞ x 11. 26358-4

CAPTURED BY THE INDIANS: 15 Firsthand Accounts, 1750-1870, Frederick Drimmer. Astounding true historical accounts of grisly torture, bloody conflicts, relentless pursuits, miraculous escapes and more, by people who lived to tell the tale. 384pp. 5⅜ x 8½. 24901-8

THE WORLD'S GREAT SPEECHES (Fourth Enlarged Edition), Lewis Copeland, Lawrence W. Lamm, and Stephen J. McKenna. Nearly 300 speeches provide public speakers with a wealth of updated quotes and inspiration–from Pericles' funeral oration and William Jennings Bryan's "Cross of Gold Speech" to Malcolm X's powerful words on the Black Revolution and Earl of Spenser's tribute to his sister, Diana, Princess of Wales. 944pp. 5⅜ x 8⅜. 40903-1

THE BOOK OF THE SWORD, Sir Richard F. Burton. Great Victorian scholar/adventurer's eloquent, erudite history of the "queen of weapons"–from prehistory to early Roman Empire. Evolution and development of early swords, variations (sabre, broadsword, cutlass, scimitar, etc.), much more. 336pp. 6⅛ x 9¼. 25434-8

AUTOBIOGRAPHY: The Story of My Experiments with Truth, Mohandas K. Gandhi. Boyhood, legal studies, purification, the growth of the Satyagraha (nonviolent protest) movement. Critical, inspiring work of the man responsible for the freedom of India. 480pp. 5⅜ x 8½. (Available in U.S. only.) 24593-4

CELTIC MYTHS AND LEGENDS, T. W. Rolleston. Masterful retelling of Irish and Welsh stories and tales. Cuchulain, King Arthur, Deirdre, the Grail, many more. First paperback edition. 58 full-page illustrations. 512pp. 5⅜ x 8½. 26507-2

THE PRINCIPLES OF PSYCHOLOGY, William James. Famous long course complete, unabridged. Stream of thought, time perception, memory, experimental methods; great work decades ahead of its time. 94 figures. 1,391pp. 5⅜ x 8½. 2-vol. set.
Vol. I: 20381-6   Vol. II: 20382-4

THE WORLD AS WILL AND REPRESENTATION, Arthur Schopenhauer. Definitive English translation of Schopenhauer's life work, correcting more than 1,000 errors, omissions in earlier translations. Translated by E. F. J. Payne. Total of 1,269pp. 5⅜ x 8½. 2-vol. set.
Vol. 1: 21761-2   Vol. 2: 21762-0

MAGIC AND MYSTERY IN TIBET, Madame Alexandra David-Neel. Experiences among lamas, magicians, sages, sorcerers, Bonpa wizards. A true psychic discovery. 32 illustrations. 321pp. 5⅜ x 8½. (Available in U.S. only.) 22682-4

THE EGYPTIAN BOOK OF THE DEAD, E. A. Wallis Budge. Complete reproduction of Ani's papyrus, finest ever found. Full hieroglyphic text, interlinear transliteration, word-for-word translation, smooth translation. 533pp. 6½ x 9¼. 21866-X

MATHEMATICS FOR THE NONMATHEMATICIAN, Morris Kline. Detailed, college-level treatment of mathematics in cultural and historical context, with numerous exercises. Recommended Reading Lists. Tables. Numerous figures. 641pp. 5⅜ x 8½. 24823-2

PROBABILISTIC METHODS IN THE THEORY OF STRUCTURES, Isaac Elishakoff. Well-written introduction covers the elements of the theory of probability from two or more random variables, the reliability of such multivariable structures, the theory of random function, Monte Carlo methods of treating problems incapable of exact solution, and more. Examples. 502pp. 5⅜ x 8½. 40691-1

THE RIME OF THE ANCIENT MARINER, Gustave Doré, S. T. Coleridge. Doré's finest work; 34 plates capture moods, subtleties of poem. Flawless full-size reproductions printed on facing pages with authoritative text of poem. "Beautiful. Simply beautiful."–*Publisher's Weekly.* 77pp. 9¼ x 12. 22305-1

NORTH AMERICAN INDIAN DESIGNS FOR ARTISTS AND CRAFTSPEOPLE, Eva Wilson. Over 360 authentic copyright-free designs adapted from Navajo blankets, Hopi pottery, Sioux buffalo hides, more. Geometrics, symbolic figures, plant and animal motifs, etc. 128pp. 8⅜ x 11. (Not for sale in the United Kingdom.) 25341-4

SCULPTURE: Principles and Practice, Louis Slobodkin. Step-by-step approach to clay, plaster, metals, stone; classical and modern. 253 drawings, photos. 255pp. 8⅛ x 11. 22960-2

THE INFLUENCE OF SEA POWER UPON HISTORY, 1660–1783, A. T. Mahan. Influential classic of naval history and tactics still used as text in war colleges. First paperback edition. 4 maps. 24 battle plans. 640pp. 5⅜ x 8½. 25509-3

THE STORY OF THE TITANIC AS TOLD BY ITS SURVIVORS, Jack Winocour (ed.). What it was really like. Panic, despair, shocking inefficiency, and a little heroism. More thrilling than any fictional account. 26 illustrations. 320pp. 5⅜ x 8½. 20610-6

FAIRY AND FOLK TALES OF THE IRISH PEASANTRY, William Butler Yeats (ed.). Treasury of 64 tales from the twilight world of Celtic myth and legend: "The Soul Cages," "The Kildare Pooka," "King O'Toole and his Goose," many more. Introduction and Notes by W. B. Yeats. 352pp. 5⅜ x 8½. 26941-8

BUDDHIST MAHAYANA TEXTS, E. B. Cowell and others (eds.). Superb, accurate translations of basic documents in Mahayana Buddhism, highly important in history of religions. The Buddha-karita of Asvaghosha, Larger Sukhavativyuha, more. 448pp. 5⅜ x 8½. 25552-2

ONE TWO THREE . . . INFINITY: Facts and Speculations of Science, George Gamow. Great physicist's fascinating, readable overview of contemporary science: number theory, relativity, fourth dimension, entropy, genes, atomic structure, much more. 128 illustrations. Index. 352pp. 5⅜ x 8½. 25664-2

EXPERIMENTATION AND MEASUREMENT, W. J. Youden. Introductory manual explains laws of measurement in simple terms and offers tips for achieving accuracy and minimizing errors. Mathematics of measurement, use of instruments, experimenting with machines. 1994 edition. Foreword. Preface. Introduction. Epilogue. Selected Readings. Glossary. Index. Tables and figures. 128pp. 5⅜ x 8½. 40451-X

DALÍ ON MODERN ART: The Cuckolds of Antiquated Modern Art, Salvador Dalí. Influential painter skewers modern art and its practitioners. Outrageous evaluations of Picasso, Cézanne, Turner, more. 15 renderings of paintings discussed. 44 calligraphic decorations by Dalí. 96pp. 5⅜ x 8½. (Available in U.S. only.) 29220-7

ANTIQUE PLAYING CARDS: A Pictorial History, Henry René D'Allemagne. Over 900 elaborate, decorative images from rare playing cards (14th–20th centuries): Bacchus, death, dancing dogs, hunting scenes, royal coats of arms, players cheating, much more. 96pp. 9¼ x 12¼. 29265-7

MAKING FURNITURE MASTERPIECES: 30 Projects with Measured Drawings, Franklin H. Gottshall. Step-by-step instructions, illustrations for constructing handsome, useful pieces, among them a Sheraton desk, Chippendale chair, Spanish desk, Queen Anne table and a William and Mary dressing mirror. 224pp. 8⅛ x 11¼. 29338-6

THE FOSSIL BOOK: A Record of Prehistoric Life, Patricia V. Rich et al. Profusely illustrated definitive guide covers everything from single-celled organisms and dinosaurs to birds and mammals and the interplay between climate and man. Over 1,500 illustrations. 760pp. 7½ x 10⅛. 29371-8